EVENTS THAT SHAPED
THE NATION

EVENTS THAT SHAPED SHAPED THE NATION

By Rick Phalen

PELICAN PUBLISHING COMPANY
Gretna 2001

The word "Pelican" and the depiction of a pelican are trademarks of Pelican Publishing Company, Inc., and are registered in the U.S. Patent and Trademark Office.

Library of Congress Cataloging-in-Publication Data

Events that shaped the nation / [compiled] by Rick Phalen.
    p. cm.
    Includes index.
    ISBN 1-56554-935-X (alk. paper)
    1. United States—History—1945- 2. World War, 1939-1945—
United States. 3. United States—Social conditions—1945-
4. United States—Biography. 5. Interviews—United States.
I. Phalen, Richard C., 1937-

E742 .E85 2001
973.9—dc21

                                          2001036914

Printed in the United States of America
Published by Pelican Publishing Company, Inc.
1000 Burmaster Street, Gretna, Louisiana 70053

*To Kathleen and Shawn, no finer daughters,
and to my mother,
who introduced me to history*

I don't think we'll ever be done with Pearl Harbor. I think Pearl Harbor is like Gettysburg, Appomattox, Lincoln's assassination, like Yorktown and the surrender to General Washington. God help our country if it's ever forgotten.

—Stephen Ambrose

Contents

Part II: This Is the Beginning of the End (Tallyrand)

Part III: The Last Hurrah (Edwin O'Connor)

Part IV: Difficulty Is the Excuse History Never Accepts (Edward R. Murrow)

Acknowledgments

As a child I was introduced by my mother to the *Book of Knowledge,* a collection of books on world history. This opened a whole new world for me and definitely shaped my life.

I was fortunate to attend fine schools in Evanston, Illinois, with gifted history and government teachers such as Teenie May Robinson, Ramona Jarvis, Chet Renner, and Clarence Kollman. Graduating from the University of Missouri with a degree in history encouraged me to delve further into American history, with primary emphasis on the Great Depression forward. Many of the historians and writers I have read for decades contributed to this book and all are as fascinating to talk with as they are to read.

Additionally, I spoke with participants in major events from Pearl Harbor to the late 1990s. Those on the playing field have different perspectives than those in the stands.

Everyone who participated was wonderful to work with and could not have been more open and forthcoming with their comments.

Events That Shaped the Nation is my fourth book and my friend and colleague Alice Vazquez has assisted me on each project. Her advice and insights are invaluable.

Introduction

Adm. Husband E. Kimmel, commander in chief, Pacific Fleet, and Lt. Gen. Walter Short, Hawaii's army commander, had scheduled a golf game for 9:30 A.M. at the army course at Fort Shafter. At 7:45 A.M. Kimmel received a phone call reporting an enemy submarine in the Pearl Harbor entry channel. A few minutes later, waiting for his driver to take him to Pearl Harbor, he witnessed Japanese bombs falling on his ships, the USS *Arizona* exploding like an enormous fireball. December 7, 1941, would indeed live in infamy.

From that moment, America forever changed. We mobilized faster than any nation in history, shedding the last remnants of the Depression, our energy directed toward the war effort. Six months later we won the Battle of Midway, the event that shaped the war in the Pacific, followed by victories at Guadalcanal, North Africa, Italy, Normandy, Guam, Saipan, Iwo Jima, Okinawa, The Bulge, Remagan, and the final surrender of Germany. Three months later, the atomic bomb would take Japan out of the war, ending World War II.

Many forecasted hard economic times for post-war America, but they were wrong. Not anticipated was the confrontation between the West and Russia, the euphoria of victory quickly turning to fear and distrust. The Iron Curtain, spies, Russia's possession of the atomic bomb, Korea, and McCarthy acidified relations between East and West. America's racial environment changed when Jackie Robinson broke the color barrier in baseball in 1947. Television by the late forties was about to take the country to another level.

Stalin died in 1953 and the Korean War ended a few months later. Ike was president and the Cold War moderated somewhat. Joe McCarthy, after ruining many lives, died of alcoholism in 1957, and after twenty-five years we took a long breath, looked at ourselves, and realized we were a different society. Benignly at first, then like its relentless beat, rock and roll changed music, and artists such as Como, Clooney, Alberts, and Sacca were quickly run over. *Brown v. Board of Education* put an end to school segregation, but it would take more than a ruling to fully implement it, as evidenced at Little Rock.

The 1960s began with anticipation and hope, but Berlin, Cuba, JFK's assassination, Vietnam, student unrest, war protestors, drugs, the King and Bobby Kennedy assassinations, and the Democratic Convention helped make this the most disruptive decade in our history. Television shaped our view of the world, not only politically but recreationally, helping to establish professional football and two figures who dominated the decade: Vince Lombardi and Muhammad Ali.

Whereas the sixties were for the most part economically prosperous, the 1970s experienced "stagflation," continued protests, Watergate, the end of the Vietnam War, Nixon's resignation, oil "shortages," and the Iranian Hostage Crisis. The Women's Movement gained momentum, and Jimmy Carter's interest in the presidency surpassed his comprehension of it.

Reagan made Americans feel good again about their country and fundamentally changed the United States-Soviet relationship. The economy strengthened and people began to hear about hardware, software, and computers—America was about to go to yet another level. George Bush, after trying to assist Gorbachev, was caught flat-footed, as was nearly everyone else, as the U.S.S.R. imploded. Marx was wrong.

Then came the Gulf War, Clinton, and unprecedented prosperity. The nineties embourgeoisement of America brought not only material gain but a culture of distrust, where "spinning"—AKA lying—became a growth industry. NOW, along with others, did a minuet around the truth to help protect Clinton in the name of expediency. "Let's get through the problem, then worry about it" was becoming the national reflex.

We entered the new century more prosperous than ever before. But though Joe DiMaggio is gone, America still turns its lonely eyes to him. We know where Joe has gone, but where are we going?

I endeavor to provide the answers through a series of personal interviews that I conducted over a nine-year period. The conversations were difficult for some participants because of the memories they elicited. Tears and anguish were not uncommon.

These interviews cover many of the crucial events that shaped the nation over the past sixty years, as participants, historians, and writers reveal America's transformation from Pearl Harbor to Bill Clinton. Are we the same people who shot at Japanese airplanes from the roof of Schofield Barracks; who prevailed at Guadalcanal, Iwo Jima, Normandy, and The Bulge; who after the Depression and the war built the foundation for our present economic strength; who laid the groundwork for the winning of the Cold War?

Events That Shaped the Nation provides the answers to these and many other questions.

EVENTS THAT SHAPED
THE NATION

PART I

One Must Be Something,
in Order to Do Something

(Goethe)

CHAPTER 1

December 7, 1941

Allen Smith

Near the conclusion of Allen's interview he began to cry. The memories of that terrible day still torment him. Americans used to tell one another, "Remember Pearl Harbor." Allen would like to forget it but never will. And America should never forget Allen Smith, a man who served his country for thirty-four years in the United States Navy.

I entered the service in June 1937 from a little village in Pennsylvania. I took my boot camp at Newport, Rhode Island, before going to sea. The destroyer I was assigned to moved from its base in San Diego, California, to the Hawaiian detachment at Pearl Harbor in November 1940. I was there a little over a year getting acquainted with the islands and destroyer maneuvering.

We all expected we would be drawn into the war. But I don't think any of us expected we were going to be jumped and to be so unprepared as we were at Pearl Harbor.

It was a different era. We didn't have radar; you couldn't see over the horizon. Everything was from your eyes out to the horizon. It was pretty embryonic. We were more or less by ourselves. We thought we would take the carriers, cruisers, and battleships and go out, line up, and fight the Japanese. We knew the Japanese would be our enemy. We figured we wouldn't be transferred back to the East Coast to fight the war in Europe.

There was radar at the northwest tip of Oahu on December 7, 1941, but it was turned off early.

Having had extensive experience with radar I can understand what happened. It was an old bedspring radar and didn't provide any definition. There was no way of identifying anything with it. All you could find was some blob on it. The return on radars in those days could have been from a thundercloud, a large electrical storm, or most anything, but the speed of the blip on the scope would tell you it wasn't a thunderstorm, that it would be aircraft.

I was lead signalman on our destroyer. I had awakened early on December 7th and came to the bridge to review the night signal traffic because we were communications guard for our nest of destroyers—three of us nested at a buoy. I reviewed all the traffic to make sure it had been routed properly and that everyone had received what they were supposed to get. That's what I was doing just before eight o'clock when one of the signalmen on the bridge hoisted the international flag prep, or preparatory, which is the signal for the execution of morning colors in the fleet.

As he hoisted the flag, the stern of the ship was pointed towards Wheeler Field and Schofield Barracks and he alerted me to aircraft activity over Schofield and Wheeler, asking me to check it out. I put a long glass on it, a big thirty-power spotting glass, and it horrified me, froze me, because the planes were Japanese and there was smoke coming up. It was quite a distance away, about five to ten miles, but you could see explosions occurring. I immediately hollered to the quartermaster—the watch on the quarterdeck—to get the OD out. I said there were Japanese aircraft over Wheeler Field.

The officer of the deck was a guy named Lieutenant Miller. He was in the wardroom, not out on the quarterdeck. The captain was in his cabin. I noticed three airplanes to my left coming from Barber's Point, so low on the cane field you could see the prop wake on the cane as they were flying toward us. They were easily identified as Japanese and had torpedoes on them. Their torpedoes were silver and the thought occurred to me of the silver bullet the masked rider used. Our torpedoes were always smeared with paraalkatone and were brown, greasy, dirty-looking things. But these were shiny and silver and I was mesmerized and didn't come to my senses until they were almost abeam of the nest of destroyers.

They were less than 100 to 150 feet away when they released the torpedoes. I couldn't figure what was going through my mind. I was slipping off into never-never land, going off into another world. You could see the pilots. There were three planes in the formation, and [the pilots] had long scarves that trailed off behind them and they all wore leather helmets and goggles and the lead pilot had a very colorful band around his helmet.

This took me out of my lethargy and I ran into the pilothouse—not thinking what I was doing, sort of an automatic thing. You are trained to act spontaneously under situations like this, and I called the skipper and I told him there were Japanese aircraft over Pearl Harbor and they were using live ammunition and we needed him on the bridge. I said, "We need you on the bridge; hurry!" I hung up on him—I didn't wait for an answer.

Of course you don't do this, you don't hang up on the skipper, but I hung up on him and tripped the general alarm immediately. You're not supposed to do that either because you must get permission from the officer of the deck. I was briefly chided about this after the whole situation was over but . . .

I was a signalman, second class, but I was the highest-ranking signalman on the signal bridge and was in charge. The only person over me was the quartermaster, who wasn't on the bridge, and, of course, the officer of the deck, who also was not on the bridge. There was no need to wait for anything—my God, the situation was clear as to what the hell was going on and I did what was necessary and alerted the ship and got people going towards general quarters stations. By the time I got back on the signal bridge, which is out in the open and behind the pilothouse, all hell had broken loose.

The whole sky was covered with airplanes. At one time they figured there were about 160 aircraft over Pearl Harbor and they were all down at masthead height firing at us. I experienced for the first time an airplane coming at me with flashing bursts. It was too spontaneous to get scared. I didn't get frightened until five to ten minutes later. Then I noticed perspiration pouring off my forehead, palms, and the back of my neck.

When you have morning colors in the fleet, it is very colorful because everybody puts the prep flag up and it's executed at exactly 0800 hours, and then your ensigns go up the staff and the Union Jack goes up at the jack stave and the larger ships with bands play the national anthem. Cruisers and ships like that will bugle colors, and smaller ships like the destroyer, the boatswain will pipe the colors on the boatswain pipe. In the middle of this melee, with planes all over and explosions around Ford Island, prep was executed, the flags went up, the bands began to play, and airplanes are flying all around.

I don't think Stephen Spielberg, Irving Berlin, or John Philip Sousa could have choreographed anything like that. But it went on like it was an everyday occurrence. Then like the *1812 Overture* all the cannons started firing. I'm still impressed—it was like a movie.

We were buoy X-11, about 500 yards west of Ford Island and north of Pearl City. We were about a thousand yards from the *Arizona*, pointed directly at her when she went up.

The captain and I were standing on the bridge with the communications officer and everybody was going to battle stations. The old man [the captain] was on the telephone talking to the boatswain's mate, telling him to make all preparations for getting the ship under way, and also talking to the chief petty officer, to put all boilers on the line and get them fired up to get under way.

I was becoming aware—for the first time in my life—of my importance. I noticed people looking at me, including the communications officer. By then I was considered an experienced bridge hand, an experienced signalman. I had a hash mark and had been a little over four years on the signal bridge.

As I said, there was no such thing as radar or radio-telephones because everything that came to the bridge came through the eyes of the signalman and through lookouts. You saw things before the skipper saw them and you got messages before the captain, and gave them to him. You became a right-hand man to the captain. You got closer to him than his officer of the deck.

Oh, God, when the *Arizona* went up the captain doubled over. He said something like, "Oh, my God." He's often talked to me about this and he doesn't really know why he said it, but he added, "I didn't know this was going to happen." It wasn't prompted by any remark. He just looked at me and said, "I didn't know this was going to happen." He's still alive; he's 101 years old. His daughters are taking care of him back in a beautiful farm in North Carolina. Wonderful man.

Then the old man told the boatswain to prepare to cast off and get under way, and reports kept coming in about manning our battle stations. The guns were up, turning, and active, and we were getting reports from the engine room that another boiler had been put on the line, and then the boatswain came back and said there were no men on the ships alongside to handle lines. The skipper told him to cut them and the lines—these big, beautiful six-inch Manila hawsers—were cut with fire axes.

A boatswain's mate third [class]—in those days we called them coxswain—went over the side and went hand over hand down the anchor chain with a sledgehammer and dropped into the water and swam over to the buoy and somehow got up on the big buoy and broke the pin on the pelican hook to let the anchor chain go free, so we could be free of the buoy and the other ships to begin our transit into the channel and out into the harbor. Breaking loose from the ships gave us room to start using the five-inch 38-caliber rifles we had on board. We didn't have any defense; we were totally unprepared. Fifty-caliber machine guns are just absolutely useless against aircraft.

I saw a B-17 get shot down. He mushed it in—pancaked into the cane fields—but I didn't see any other American aircraft in the air. We'd always been told we had the greatest air force in the world—nobody could beat us. We were trained and told you couldn't sink a battleship, and they were going down a thousand yards away. You could see what was going on over there, the horrendous noise and explosions, the black smoke, and you began to visualize people were there. They were getting blown up and maybe you're next.

The thing that impressed me was that people were looking to me. You realize you're the one that sees everything, you're the one that receives the messages, who informs the captain. You're the one the captain talks to when he wants to send something out, and you begin to realize you have a real job to do and have to look calm. A person could not do that without training, and I had four years, all of your actions become involuntary, just like wiping your nose.

We were now going out into the channel. Pearl Harbor was very restricted. It was a very small place to put a whole fleet, and the channel was only a couple of hundred yards wide. We eased away from the buoy and into the channel and commenced our journey south, out of the channel, which took us alongside Ford Island.

The *Raleigh* had been hit. The *Utah* had already rolled over and was upside down, the crew sliding off the bottom and the side into the water. They were swimming out toward our ship and wanted to get on board, but the captain said, "No, don't stop for them." Then we passed the big seaplane tender, the *Curtis*; she was on fire, a plane had crashed into her deck. The pilot took it into the hanger deck of the *Curtis* and guys were jumping off her.

Ford Island by then was just a mess of fire and black smoke and as we entered it was almost like instrument flying. We encountered black smoke so thick you couldn't see the channel. It took a bit of expert seamanship by the skipper and the quartermaster to stay in the channel. We cleared and looked back up the line of battleships and saw nearly every one of them sitting on the bottom.

When we passed Mary's Point we were then fairly clear. The battleship *Nevada* had gotten loose from the battle line; I don't know if she was told to ground herself or whether she was hit, but she was grounded off Mary's Point. It was touching. The band was playing "Maryland, My Maryland" as we went by and she dipped her colors to us. Normally, the destroyer would dip colors to the senior ship, and *Nevada* was senior to us.

It was one of those crazy things that happened in this melee; I thought it was really something. Then the signalman on their bridge flashed a message to us: "Good Hunting." Everybody by then knew we were fighting for our lives. About that time we had a run made on us by two dive bombers, but they missed. It was obvious they would like to sink something in the channel and bottle the fleet up, but they missed and we cleared the sea buoy just as the second raid was coming in.

It had been about forty-five minutes since the attack started, and I remarked to the skipper we were running away from the fight. He put his hand on my shoulder and said, "We have something else to do." I thought, *those poor bastards, they're going to get pummeled again.* You couldn't fight back in the harbor; it was too close quarters. You would be shooting your own ships and destroying everybody in sight.

The navy has an op-word, it's called "Sail." It's a coverall thing, you know exactly what you're supposed to do. So when we cleared the channel we began a full-power, 38-knot run, for about a mile and a half beyond the sea buoy. This churned the water and prevented submarines from making sonar contact and tracking ships coming out. We then turned around and came back at 5 knots listening and trying to detect whether any submarines were present. We made two runs and then started getting radio traffic. Radio traffic was very slow, and had to be decoded.

The message was to rendezvous with the *Enterprise* and the position to go to. We took off and picked up two or three destroyers along the route, and we rendezvoused with the *Enterprise*. It was now about two o'clock in the afternoon and she had a couple of cruisers with her. We struck off in a northwesterly direction, assuming that was the position of the Japanese strike force, looking for them. It's probably a good thing we didn't find them because, knowing now the size of the force, they'd have beaten us and I probably wouldn't be talking now.

At night we settled down to a zigzag course to avoid being hit by submarines and watching, thinking, and talking. It was an odd night, totally quiet, people mumbling, rehashing what each other had seen, what was going to happen next. We only had two officers on board so we had to reorganize in terms of standing watch and things like that.

We spent the next day running pretty high, somewhere between 22 and 27 knots, launching and recovering aircraft that went out looking for sightings, and then we came back Tuesday evening to Pearl Harbor and replenished. It was unbelievable to see the extent of the destruction of the ships, and fires were still burning. But we didn't stay long, We replenished and came back out with the *Lexington*. The *Lexington* had come to Pearl from whatever position she was in during the attack.

We joined *Lexington* and a tanker named *Neches,* and there were several cruisers and other destroyers and we began a high-speed run in defense of Wake Island. The *Lexington* had a group of Brewster Buffalos and some SBD dive bombers and we tried to replenish Wake Island, but the Japanese beat us back, and while in the area we received the message Wake had fallen. Lexington took a couple of cruisers and some destroyers with her and took off and we were assigned to protect the *Neches*, get her back to Midway because she had 1,500 marines on board. It was a scary voyage, given the responsibility of protecting this ship from submarine attacks.

We went back out again with the *Enterprise* and a whole battle group and made the first attack on Japanese forces in the Marshall and Gilbert Islands. That was a very successful raid, destroying a lot of their facilities and aircraft.

Pearl Harbor was a big change in your life, and people reflected back on the girls they left behind, mothers and fathers, things they wanted to do. It was a big change, everybody realized it was a new world now.

The biggest thing: most people became extremely aware of their own presence. I don't know whether I'm saying this right, but suddenly I felt, I'm no longer Allen Smith. I now have a role to play and I've got to play it correctly. I must do everything right. I could never make a mistake again, I can't disappoint the skipper. He must have complete confidence in me and I felt I have to show the men. Before, in training, if you did something wrong, you'd go back and do it again. Well, you couldn't make any more mistakes. Everything had to go perfect. Life had changed.

When I was watching [the movie] *Saving Private Ryan*, I was extremely interested in the story because these were guys like me. They were professional military men and they were really working a problem to find this guy. They showed twenty-five minutes of people being killed, the slaughter that went on on the beach, and I was amazed it didn't bother me.

I saw the tragedy and the horror, but I guarantee you, Rick, you show me one live picture of Pearl Harbor and it just goes through me, 'cause I see myself. All of a sudden I'm in that picture and nobody can see me. I can see myself in it and I get nervous. Even now my voice begins to chatter a little bit when I visualize the scene that I was actually in . . . excuse me.

See, I had enough presence of mind to get a glass of water. I don't know whether that explains it . . .

I frequently get calls to speak about Pearl Harbor, particularly to naval groups and Kiwanis clubs and things like that, usually around Pearl Harbor Day. I try to avoid them if I can because, honestly, I've tried to forget it. They say "Remember Pearl Harbor," but there really isn't anything I would rather do than to forget the whole damn thing. I don't need that kind of motivation to give me the courage to defend my country if it should ever happen again.

CHAPTER 2

Guadalcanal

Ken Todd

One of the most important battles of World War II was fought in the Solomon Islands at Guadalcanal. Ken Todd was there.

I was commissioned a second lieutenant in June 1932 from ROTC at the University of North Dakota. The War Department [it was the War Department at that time] asked for twelve infantry volunteers, company grade, to go to Hawaii. Since I was a first lieutenant I volunteered, and was accepted.

We were ordered to report to the port of embarkation at San Francisco on June 3, 1941, and went over the 24th of June, and our wives came later on another ship. My wife and I couldn't get quarters at Schofield Barracks and had to go elsewhere. There was a little town about two miles from Schofield called Wahiawa and we rented a small house there, and that's where we were living at the time of the attack.

It was about five minutes to eight when we heard planes over the roof of our house; [they] just about touched the house. We went outside and saw the red circles on the bottoms of the planes. They flew directly to Wheeler Field and we saw puffs of smoke from Wheeler, so we knew they were bombing the air base.

We turned on the radio and the first thing we heard was: *All military personnel report to their stations immediately. The Island of Oahu is under Japanese attack.* I dressed as quickly as I could, got in the car, and started toward Schofield. They were strafing the streets and houses. I had a light car and I didn't get hit, but the car in front of me and the car in back of me each got a bullet hole.

31

I got to Schofield and everything was bedlam, pandemonium and confusion. We didn't know what to do because all our weapons and ammunition were locked in the storeroom. We had to break into the storeroom to get the machine guns, got a couple on the roof of the headquarters quadrangle and started firing at the planes. I don't recall that we hit anything.

After about twenty minutes those planes flew away; about an hour later more planes came back and dropped bombs and did more strafing of Schofield Barracks. When they bombed Wheeler Field they hit the buildings and destroyed all the fighter planes; they also hit the mess hall and a lot of soldiers were killed and wounded. It's hard to describe. Just hell, that's all.

We got all the women and children together and bused them down to Honolulu, into the Punch Bowl. They opened up some schools to receive the women and children. They were there for two or three days until things quieted down and then they returned to Schofield.

My wife accompanied the women down to Honolulu and went by Pearl Harbor. She was in an army truck with the back open and saw Pearl Harbor in flames. She said it was the worst sight she ever saw. She'll never forget that.

After Pearl Harbor we began jungle training because they expected to send the Twenty-fifth Division to Guadalcanal. We trained for six months, and in November '42 our division was sent to Guadalcanal to relieve the First Marine Division.

I was there from November '42 until about April '43, when I was transferred to the headquarters of the Fourteenth Corps. We moved on to New Georgia and then on to Bougainville, taking one island at a time. I was over there three years and was the second person to be rotated when they began the rotation policy. Only one person had been there longer than I had.

Guadalcanal was the biggest turning point. It took six months to take Guadalcanal. We never knew how long we'd be there because the Japs were strong, and they wanted Guadalcanal in the worst way . . . they knew if they lost it that that would be the turning point and that's what happened; we secured the island on February 9, 1943.

At the end, the Japanese escaped from the northwest part of the island.

That is correct. I was personnel officer of the regiment and was in the rear echelon. On an island, rear echelon isn't much further behind than the forward echelon. On February 1, 1943, I got a phone call from the Twenty-fifth Infantry Division Headquarters and was told to get my unit to a certain point. We formed a defensive line in the rear echelon, figuring the Japs would make one last attack. We even had the company clerks out there on the line.

The colonel inspected our unit after we had dug in, then came up to me and said, "Captain Todd, you will defend this line to the last man. You will hold this line to the last man."

I said, "Yes, Sir," saluted, and he was gone.

That was on the first of February, and on the nights of the second and third, the Japs had about 15,000 troops. We thought they were going to attack. What they were doing was boarding destroyers and getting out of there, the whole 15,000 evacuated in a couple of nights on destroyers that came in and took them away.

Some people said the Japanese couldn't shoot. We found they could shoot very accurately and were good soldiers, trained to fight 'til the death. We were fed better than the Japanese because we were receiving supplies and they weren't, making it very difficult for the Japanese to fight. And of course there was a lot of malaria and sickness. Every day people on both sides went down with those tropical diseases. It was just terrible.

The marines did a great job of invading and holding the island.

Oh, just terrific. General Vandergrift was a great general and inspired his men. They stacked the Japs in piles when they attacked, trying to take Henderson Field. They had to take bulldozers and bulldoze them into big ditches at the end of the battle.

Guadalcanal definitely was the turning point in the war.

CHAPTER 3

Midway

Tom O'Reilly

Midway Island is located 1,300 miles northwest of Honolulu and comprises a land area of only two square miles. In June 1942, a Japanese naval force of sixty-five destroyers, twenty-two heavy cruises, eleven battleships, twenty-one submarines, and four aircraft carriers with seven hundred planes and eighty troop transports attempted to take Midway.

We had broken the Japanese code and were deciphering their messages almost as fast as they were sending them. Having this element working for us, our smaller force of seven heavy cruisers, one light cruiser, fourteen destroyers, twelve submarines, and four aircraft carriers intercepted them, beat them, and changed the course of history.

I arrived at Kaneohe Naval Air Station in February 1941. It was a sea-plane base for PBYs. At the time of the attack I was an aerographers mate 2nd class. Our function was to support the PBYs on reconnaissance. There was a pattern we would fly, a sector like a piece of pie. We had a weatherman—an aerographer is a weatherman—on each flight because we had limited weather information and this supplemented our other information.

The aerographer would sit in the blister and operate the machine guns if it was necessary, but he was there primarily for observation, not as a gunner. We had been crudely trained in aerial gunnery and in recognizing the various Japanese airplanes. This was the routine from the time we arrived to the time the war started.

On the morning of the Pearl Harbor attack I was in my barracks on the second floor and I heard a tremendous commotion outside. I thought it was a fight, a Sunday morning brawl between the marines and the navy, a common occurrence with hangovers and such. I ran out to take a look and a plane went by my window, not more than fifty feet away. I could see the red ball, but it didn't make any sense and I thought the army—the army was the air force in those days—was having a drill. It only took a few seconds to realize it wasn't a drill, because shells were exploding all over and the hangers were being bombed.

I got in a truck and went down to the hangers to see what we could salvage, but everything was on fire and I realized there wasn't anything to salvage. So I turned around and ran to the armory to get a rifle. Unfortunately there were only fifty rifles that weren't in cosmoline, a thick grease used to protect firearms, and it takes an awful lot of work to clean them. I grabbed one of the rifles and ran back to the administration building. Two friends—one a radioman, the other a 1st class aerographer—were observing what was going on.

The second attack was in progress. The last plane in the attack circled the harbor, then came directly at us at about 100 feet. The three of us got off a shot. Whether anyone else was firing, I don't know, but the plane went into a hill behind us. It turned out this was the squadron commander, and he was probably making a reconnaissance but was shot down. There is a plaque there now and the man was a lieutenant Iidea.

There was tremendous excitement because of the possibility of invasion and the fact we didn't have any aircraft on the base. In the navy, the battleship was considered the supreme ship. So when we got word that the battleships had gone down, we were absolutely dumbfounded and were sure we were going to be invaded.

The next couple of weeks was chaos. They dug pits all over the base and put in what machine guns they could, and if during the night a rabbit ran across the field all you heard was "brrrrrr." Everybody was so jittery. The morning after the attack we were ordered to take all our clothes and place them in vats of coffee; this was our camouflage. They dyed all our clothes in coffee; of course it smelled good.

Radar was in its infancy so we were the main eyes and ears of the navy. If you took us as the center and divided up the 360 degrees into sectors, as I mentioned, [like] a piece of pie, you get an idea of how we secured and protected the area so we wouldn't be hit. This was our main defense, and we flew out of Kaneohe about 800 miles, about a 1,600-mile roundtrip. This was the daily routine.

We were not advised we had cracked the Japanese [Purple] Code, and there was a strong suspicion an attack was going to be made at Midway. It was a closely guarded secret through the war that we had broken the code. They would not even let us make any entry in our flight logs referring to anything.

Now the question was: The Japanese fleet was missing and where were they headed? There was a general feeling among the code-breakers that they were somewhere in the central Pacific, and we finally concluded they were headed for Midway. The Japanese plan was to attack Midway and draw the American fleet out, then sink the fleet since the Japanese fleet was superior in numbers and airplanes. To confirm our suspicions, we decided to send an open message to Pearl Harbor from Midway saying we had concerns regarding our water supply. The Japanese code came back that AF was having problems with their water. That confirmed our suspicions that the destination was Midway since they knew in coding that AF was Midway.

The planes that found the Japanese fleet came from Kaneohe, doing sector searches, and one of them spotted the fleet and notified Pearl Harbor.

The Japanese felt they could completely cripple our fleet, realizing the carriers were the key. They knew we had very little left, only the Enterprise and the Hornet, and they considered the Yorktown so badly damaged it couldn't take part in any attack. So the strategy was to totally eliminate our navy and then proceed to Australia or wherever they chose. Midway became the most significant battle of the war, Japan being an island nation [that] depended on its fleet to protect it and its supply routes. Therefore, eliminating the American fleet was its main strategy.

Admiral Nimitz decided this was a great opportunity to position ourselves and attack them at the most vulnerable time when they were either coming back for refueling or when they were empty and in the process of making a changeover. We had the *Hornet,* the *Enterprise,* and *Yorktown* in position to attack the Japanese carriers when they were at their most vulnerable, and we were able to sink all four of their major carriers and damage other parts of their fleet.

In the fighting the Japanese were able to find the *Yorktown,* and damaged it sufficiently so that the next day we had to torpedo it since we couldn't tow it back to Pearl Harbor. The net effect was we destroyed the fighting ability of the Japanese navy with their loss of four carriers, and they never fully recovered from it. Definitely [it was] the turning point in the war in the Pacific.

I have worked with the Japanese since the war. One of my very close friends was on one of those two-man submarines. Another that I was very close to was a graduate of the Japanese Naval Academy and he was sunk twice during the war.

One of the astonishing things is how they feel about the bombing of Hiroshima. I never found a Japanese my age who wasn't convinced that it was the only thing that saved Japan, since our fire bombing was far worse than the atomic bomb. It took this catastrophic situation to bring the emperor to oppose the army's reluctance to surrender.

Pearl Harbor made me think, *How did this happen? What brought this about?* I thought, *If I live through this war, I'm going to be an active citizen and not a bystander.* After the war I graduated from Colgate University with a major in political science.

I have spent the remainder of my life actively involved in government activity, including running for congress in New York in 1956, but not winning. I have continued to this day being active in what's happening in our government and in world affairs.

CHAPTER 4

Iwo Jima

James Bradley

Iwo Jima is a two-mile-by-five-mile volcanic island lying halfway between Saipan and Japan that held tremendous military significance for the United States during World War II. We needed the island because it housed a radar station that gave mainland Japan a two-hour early warning of our approaching bombers, and afforded a base for Japanese fighters to attack these B-29 bombers going to and coming back from Japan.

In fact, Iwo Jima-based Japanese planes destroyed more B-29s on the ground on Tinian and Saipan than were lost on all the bombing raids on Tokyo. Also, by taking the island, the B-29s could land there, change crews, transfer the wounded, and fuel. It also afforded P-51 fighters the opportunity to accompany the bombers to their targets.

The marines took the island, but at a tremendous cost. They lost 6,421 men, with 19,000 wounded. The marines fought for forty-three months during World War II, yet in the month required to take Iwo Jima they suffered one-third of their total fatalities. Twenty-seven Medals of Honor were awarded.

It made the difference. A total of 2,400 distressed B-29s, with 25,000 crewmen, made life-saving landings on Iwo Jima.

James Bradley is the author of the bestselling book *Flags of Our Fathers*. It is one of the finest accounts of World War II ever written.

> When you go home
> Tell them for us and say
> For your tomorrow
> We gave our today
> —Message written outside a marine ceme-
> tery on Iwo Jima by an unknown soldier.

We had to take Iwo Jima because of its locale. We had our B-29s—fantastically expensive airplanes—based in Saipan and Tinian, and unlike Europe, the Pacific was an island war, so you had to rely on whatever island rocks you could get.

Based in Tinian and Saipan, those planes bombed Japan, but had to fly over or near Iwo Jima; there was no other way because of the fuel situation. When they flew near Iwo Jima, a radar station there gave Japan two hours notice. Also, Iwo Jima-based aircraft would come up and pick off the lumbering B-29s and also get them on the way back after being damaged bombing Japan. So to continue the assault on Japan, Iwo Jima had to be taken. After taking Iwo Jima, it was estimated that it saved 25,000 lives.

The United States Army Air Force bombed Iwo Jima for seventy-two consecutive days. This was the most heavily bombed spot in the entire Pacific war. Then the navy came in and lobbed shells the weight of Volkswagens against the island; the military commanders thought they could obliterate anything and everything on the island. There was only one problem; they didn't realize the Japanese were not *on* Iwo Jima. They were *in* Iwo Jima.

You can walk around downtown Toronto—looks like a typical modern city—but since it's very cold there, Toronto built an underground city. Underground you can go to a five-star restaurant, a movie theater, dry cleaners, do your shopping—all without the snow and blustery wind. Think of Iwo Jima as something like that, a complete artificial underground city. They had fifteen miles of tunnels on a five-mile-long island with 1,500 killing rooms.

I was in the Japanese hospital on Iwo Jima—forty-five feet below rock. An atomic bomb dropped on Iwo Jima is not going to disturb anything forty-five feet below solid rock. So the marines, basically teenagers and guys in their early twenties, hit the island on February 19, 1945, and had to fight an enemy they could not see. Bullets, mortar fire, anti-aircraft guns, [and] tank fire were coming at them but they couldn't see anybody firing. It was as if the rocks and the mountains were alive with gunfire.

We took some Japanese prisoners. About 1,000 surrendered. Most were Korean laborers who didn't want to be there in the first place. They were slave laborers. The Japanese that "surrendered" generally had . . . hole[s] in their bod[ies], with blood draining out, and were unconscious, unable to move. The Japanese just did not surrender in World War II.

Flag raisings are very common [in war]. We put flags up in Normandy, Paris, Sicily, Saipan, [the] Philippines. When you conquer a territory you put your flag up. Mount Suribachi was the high ground on Iwo Jima, so the job of the Twenty-eighth Regiment, of which my dad was a part, was to cut the neck of the island and take Suribachi. In five days of horrible fighting they subdued Mount Suribachi.

In the first flag raising, the photographer interacted with the flag raisers and suggested poses; this was an extremely important photograph and extremely important flag raising. It was the first flag to go up over Japanese soil in 4,000 years. Iwo Jima, unlike Saipan or Tinian, was for a long time part of Japan itself. The mayor of Tokyo was the mayor of Iwo Jima, so this was really the invasion of Japan. It was like the capture of Hawaii or Key West. So that first flag raising was the important flag raising that day.

The second flag raising, also on February 23rd—there were eventually three throughout the battle—was one of the most insignificant events in the history of warfare. It was a replacement flag. Col. Chandler Johnson wanted the first flag as a souvenir. He understood the historical symbolism of that flag and ordered it taken down for the battalion safe. They needed another flag, so he ordered a replacement, and they lowered the first flag simultaneously with the raising of the second one.

The second flag raising was a non-event to the marines on the island. Nobody watched, nobody cheered. It was meaningless, like putting a replacement football in a football game or screwing a new light bulb into a socket. But Joe Rosenthal [an Associated Press photographer] happened to click a shot that back in the United States represented final victory, though it wasn't. The significance of the second flag raising has more to do with what happened in people's minds in the United States than what it represented on the island that day.

The second flag survived. It's in the Marine Corps Museum along with the first flag. Back in the United States, which flag would we have immediately saved? The second one. That was a relic, an icon. But on the island, the second one was only a replacement flag, not worthy of protection. It sat up there getting chewed up by the wind, no one paying attention to it. It was only the perception back in the United States that made the second flag raising have any importance at all.

The fighting began on D-Day, but the Twenty-eighth Regiment, whose actions I detail in my book [*Flags of Our Fathers*], went south, the opposite way, and conquered Suribachi. In the book there's that gung ho shot of them all waving victoriously. They captured the high ground and logically thought the battle was over. But for the Twenty-eighth Regiment, the worst was yet to come, as they went into the northern battlefields, the battle lasting until March 26—thirty-six days of fighting.

This is a fabulous photo that still sends chills down people's spines. It was sent back to the United States. People fell in love with it. It's really that simple. To me, it's a photo of my dad [John Bradley]—a guy struggling with a pipe. But to many it represents eternal American values. The photograph generates a lot of emotion. It is very interesting that the flag they raised was taken from a disabled boat at Pearl Harbor on December 7th. Then the flag rises atop Mount Suribachi four years later and becomes a symbol of hope.

The battle was over and there were no marines on the island when the [three living] flag raisers were ordered back to the United States by FDR. They were not taken from their buddies, not taken from the field of battle. Ira Hayes and Rene Gagnon were on a transport ship, the *Winged Arrow*, making their way back to Camp Tarawa on the big island of Hawaii.

When Roosevelt ordered the flag raisers back for the Seventh Bond Tour, they didn't know who was dead, who was alive. The three other flag raisers were buried at Iwo Jima, my dad was in a hospital with shrapnel throughout both his legs, and Ira and Rene were on the transport ship.

You have three guys just taken from a hell where they had lost many of their buddies. They came back and were seen as heroes, but they hadn't done anything worthy of mention. They had put up a pipe, with a flag, and to them it was an insignificant act. They understood they were doing a very important thing by being on this bond tour, and Americans pledged $26.3 billion to fight the war, almost half the 1946 U.S. budget of $56 billion.

The bond tour went from May through July 4th 1945. After that, Rene Gagnon went to Tsingtao, China, John Bradley returned to Bethesda for additional operations, and when the war ended, Ira Hayes was at Camp Tarawa training for the invasion [of Japan].

My dad told me more than he told anybody else, maybe thirty-three sentences that took him three to four hours over a period of thirty years. When I say I have the most information, it was just a sentence here and there. I bugged him the most.

When I started my search, I called my dad's buddies who were on Iwo Jima and asked them how he could have been so silent. I'm almost embarrassed by the naïvete of that question. How could he have talked?

Let's say you're in a building with thirty people you know and I attack it with shells, napalm, machine-gun fire, and two out of three are killed or wounded. You see people you know screaming as they burn alive. When you shoot someone's head off with a mortar, the pressure of the blood system goes up thirty-five feet. Then you get out of the building, you're a survivor, but you get out by crawling over the entrails of a friend who you had lunch with and his body is still shaking.

After experiencing that, it's not cocktail conversation. There is a reason these guys didn't talk. People say, "Oh, that was a very modest generation. That was a quiet generation." I don't buy that at all. You take any generation, any friendly person, and put them through a few days of horror where their best buddies are mutilated and screaming to death. I don't think there's anything to talk about. My dad probably held 200 young boys in his arms as they died, and when young boys died on Iwo Jima, they writhed in pain.

I was at the location where Ira Hayes died. I stood there with his brother, Kenny. He died face down, dead drunk, in a pool of his own vomit and blood. He had been playing cards, was drunk, got into a shoving match with a fellow Pima, and was found face down. Kenny is confident that that fight killed Ira, and whether Ira was hit on the head, [was] pushed, or tripped, the key is that he couldn't get up. He couldn't stand up after falling down.

Rene Gagnon died in the boiler room of an apartment complex where he was the janitor. Another janitor, Frank Burpee, went down to the boiler room and could not open the boiler room door. So he got a crowbar and pried it open, and there was Rene Gagnon lying dead of a heart attack. He had the inside door nob in his hand. Apparently he had pulled it off as he struggled in the throes of his heart attack.

My dad died of a stroke. My mother was watering the flowers in the sunroom. She came into the kitchen, saw him lying on the floor and wondered why he chose that moment to exercise. Then she looked at his mouth and saw some spittle and realized that something had happened. The EMS guys were there within minutes. He never regained consciousness, and died two days later, at 2:12 A.M., on Tuesday, January 11, 1994. He was seventy.

My dad took a look at Iwo Jima, and it was not something he wanted to remember, and [he] just shut it out . . . you know he cried in his sleep for four years after Iwo Jima. It was very painful for him. Then the idea of [his] being a hero because of a photo didn't make any sense to him after what he had seen. He always told me the true heroes of Iwo Jima were the guys that didn't come back.

Iwo Jima was key. With Japanese in control of it, we would not have been able to bomb Japan into submission. We never could have sent the atomic flyers to Japan with Iwo Jima endangering them. So it was critical. In terms of World War II, it's the most significant event in the history of mankind.

You might think that's an exaggeration, but if you look at all the changes—the complete shuffling of the diplomatic deck, countries going away, others rising, 70 to 100 million deaths, the dawn of a new science, of penicillin, radar, the entering of the atomic age, the dawning of the century of the Pacific—in terms of human numbers and human changes, this is the most significant event in history. That's a big turning point.

As far as the flag raising, yes, it affected John, Rene, and Ira, being in the spotlight, being called heroes, but I think the battle of Iwo Jima had much more effect. My dad did not cry in his sleep for four years because of the actresses he had to kiss on the bond tour. Ira Hayes did not have his alcohol problem because of the number of autographs he had to give. It was because so many good buddies didn't come back.

CHAPTER 5

Slugging It Out on Iwo Jima

George Gentile

For George Gentile, and other Iwo Jima survivors, their turning point occurred over forty years after the battle.

When I heard the report of the bombing of Pearl Harbor, I was in a study room at Niagara University in my second year of college. Four or us were studying while listening to the radio. We didn't know where it was located. As the reports kept coming in, we began to realize the seriousness of it and the next day President Roosevelt declared war.

Most of us within the next three or four days decided to enlist. We had to hitchhike from Niagara University to Buffalo, about thirty-forty miles, 'cause there was no enlistment office in Niagara Falls, where the school was located. I enlisted in the marines.

The Marine Corps sent me to Officers Candidate School. I was five-feet-six, and the Marine Corps had strict requirements for officers; one was height. I participated in the entire twelve weeks of Officers Candidate School, and the night before we were to graduate about six of us were called in and told we weren't going to graduate. As you can imagine, it was very, very disappointing. I had passed all of the academic subjects, the training, the rifle range, and all the other tests. The reason they gave was "command presence."

The next day we got together and in commiserating with each other realized we were all around five-feet-six or -seven. We began to realize what they meant by "command presence." I then went to Camp Lejeune and got into a replacement battalion. Most of my OCS class ended up as second lieutenants at Iwo Jima. The percentage of deaths among second lieutenants was very high at Iwo Jima. When I think of turning points, that failure through OCS probably saved my life.

The base camp for the Fourth Marine Division was in Maui in the Hawaiian Islands and that's where I was sent, put in the Thirtieth Replacement Battalion and . . . sent to Iwo Jima.

Traveling across the Pacific, the ocean seemed endless. We were all young kids, never been anywhere in our lives, had lived through the Depression. The farthest I'd been was New York City or Connecticut. There was a ship's library [where] I met a marine who also did a lot of reading. We became very friendly. My friend asked me if I would witness his will. I was naive and didn't think it was necessary to make a will.

We woke up February 19th about 4 A.M. and they served us steak and eggs. We joked about serving us our last meal, 'cause we never got steak and eggs all the time we were in the Marine Corps. When we got to Iwo, we went up topside and there were 800 American ships, the most awesome thing I have ever viewed. All across the ocean you felt alone, then we met in that large ocean that morning— all done in the darkness of night.

What a morale booster that was to see our ships there. We were told who was going to make the landing and being replacements we figured we wouldn't make the initial landing. I was assigned to a hold down deep in the ship to unload fifty-five-gallon fuel drums for the mechanized equipment. They wanted to make sure it reached the beach soon after the vehicles got on the beach.

That's what I did the first day, unloaded those fuel oil drums. They'd go up on a crane that was attached to the top deck and over the side of the ship to a boat which would take the fifty-five-gallon drums onto the beach. The second day I got bored with it and asked, "How about going in with you? I'll help unload on the beach." I went and it was complete chaos. That's the only way I can describe it.

A lot of our vehicles were swamped in the water. It was complete disorganization because so many men and equipment were coming in simultaneously. Beachmasters were assigned to keep things going, and you could see they were very, very uptight. They were screaming and yelling at different groups as to where to go and how to go, to get the swamped vehicles and boats upright and moved. It was chaos and already quite a few wounded and dead [were] on the beach—our wounded and dead.

I went back to the ship; they wouldn't allow me to stay. I think it was the third or fourth day. Things got fuzzy after that. I was sent in to replace casualties. You're a replacement, assigned to a unit within the active division. It was late in the afternoon and the officer in charge said they would assign me in the morning, so dig a foxhole and at dawn . . . report to him. During the course of trying to find out what unit we were attached to, mortars were dropping. We had our own artillery fire going over our heads and ships' fire. It was really hard to get yourself organized.

I met my friend from the ship—I called him "Izzy," that was a nickname. He had gone in earlier because he was company clerk; the company clerk keeps records of the unit. He had an attache case and a little portable typewriter and he said to me, "Do you have a foxhole anywhere for the night?"

I said, "No." I told him I'd just got onto the beach.

He said, "I have a foxhole so why don't you join me?"

I said, "Great."

In the confusion, he led me to a disabled tank. Underneath the tank he had dug a foxhole, which to me, this is my first battle—was great protection. Little did we realize we were being watched by the Japanese, because they had an eagle-eye view of everything going on from Mount Suribachi. Izzy and I were there less than an hour when mortars started dropping around us. Big mortars. Eighty-millimeter mortars.

The first time we thought it was just accidental that they landed near our tank. We're starting to feel the concussions from them. Then we decided there was fuel in the tank. If they made a direct hit, we could be burned alive. We began to run, and as we ran, the mortars followed us down the beach. I can still hear the zing of a piece of shrapnel going by my ear.

They knew how to "step it up," step up the height trajectory to keep up with you. Izzy was behind me, but I was like a bouncing ball. You'd hear the mortar before it hit. If you were fast enough, you hit the ground and might save yourself from flying shrapnel; that's what I was doing, bouncing up and down like a bouncing ball. That's how rapid the mortar fire was coming at us. When I finally got to the beach, the mortar fire stopped—probably [we were] out of their range. I looked for Izzy but couldn't find him. I went back to the tank to make sure he didn't go back there. I ended up sleeping on the beach, dug a little hole in the sand.

The following morning I was assigned to a unit and we were lining up to go to the front. One of my friends said to me, "Did you hear what happened to Izzy?"

I said, "No."

He said, "Well, they found his dog tags."

This means he was so badly blown up that that's how they were able to determine who he was. I knew then I was in the battle.

I had been hardened the first night. It's amazing how fast you become hardened when confronted with the enemy at close range; the only thing you think about is self-preservation. I forgot about Izzy completely, which was good in a way. It didn't bother me too much because you had to be prepared to take care of yourself. You overcome the tragedies that happen, self-preservation rises above it all, and you focus on saving yourself.

When they raised the flag, we realized its strategic importance, but we had no idea of its historical importance. It was just something we thought we had to do, and that was it. But it was a morale booster— a big morale booster. I was with the Fourth Marine Division on the northern end of the island, quite a distance from Mount Suribachi. For a small island we were probably as far away as you could get, at the other end of the beach, and at that time we were in a very, very serious fighting situation with the Japanese. That end of the island is filled with ravines and caves, and a lot of the Japanese were hidden in these ravines and caves, and we were having a tough time.

We didn't have much time to think about what they were doing on the other end of the island—raising the flag on Mount Suribachi. It wasn't until the battle was completely over—I'm talking about March 16th—that I realized the importance of it.

We were told the island was secured officially. Actually, it wasn't, but the people back home were getting so upset with all the casualties our government wanted to let them know we were victorious. But we had as many casualties after the island was officially secured. But March 16th they told us it was officially secured. We were going to board ship the following day, but on the way back we had to mop up. Mopping up is going back through the territory you've already taken and mak[ing] sure no Japanese are in caves or sniper-firing at us.

That was a hairy day because you'd hate to get hit when you're going back aboard ship. We had to check the caves and if we were not sure there were any Japanese in there, we'd either throw a hand grenade in there or demolition men with high explosives would close it by blowing up the mouth of the cave. We did this the last day and finally got to the beach.

Lying on the beach was a stack of newspapers someone had dropped for us. They were bound, left for anyone who wanted to take them before getting aboard ship. On the front page was the flag raising on Mount Suribachi, a huge photo. I think it was the *New York Daily News*. I picked it up and it hit me what a great thing [had] happened at Iwo Jima. [It] was almost a month later that I realized the impact of it.

I was reminded of the part in *Flags of Our Fathers*, which James Bradley wrote, that after the battles, when we went into the caves, many of the Japanese had committed suicide. They'd hold a grenade to their stomach rather than surrender. Those not of Japanese ancestry, but laborers from countries they'd captured, didn't have that same suicidal feeling, so they were taken prisoner.

We were shipped back to Maui. They gave us five days rest and recreation in Honolulu, what they call R&R, to get back to normal after the trauma of the battle. I'll never forget that, it was such a great change from what we had been through. We stayed at the Moana Hotel next to the Royal Hawaiian.

The military had taken over all the hotels on Waikiki Beach. They had people with barbecue stoves cooking for us. It was a great five days, and then we got back to camp and, boy, they lowered the boom. We knew we were going to be the initial invaders of Japan.

When we got word of the atomic bomb, there was a feeling of elation throughout the camp, 20,000 men in a division—that's what we had on Maui. Things started to come out of the woodwork. I don't know where some of them got the bottles. It was just a celebration. I always remember from the moment we heard the news someone got the record "Oh, What A Beautiful Morning" and they played it over and over all day long. And that's what it was, a beautiful day and a beautiful feeling for us, so whenever I hear "Oh, What A Beautiful Morning," I remember back to that.

I practiced as a dentist for thirty-eight years in my hometown. I never talked about Iwo Jima to my family or friends. I was a member of the VFW, the American Legion, the Marine Corps League, but I never was active. I'd pay my dues and that was about it. I became active in local and state politics, became a member of civic clubs, the Knights of Columbus, the Elks, things like that. But I never went into my Marine Corps history with anyone, not even my family too much. If they asked me questions, I would answer them. That's about it.

In 1987 I was getting ready to retire, and a nephew who was a career man in the Marine Corps called and said, "They're having a reunion of Iwo Jima vets down on Long Island, New York. Why don't you go?"

I happened to have a patient of mine who was an Iwo Jima survivor. He came in a few days later for an appointment and I told him, "There's going to be a reunion down on Long Island, New York. You want to go?"

He called back and said, "Let's go."

It was a good time. We met some of the old buddies—not many. On the way home I got to thinking about how many of us were left. I called the Marine Corps, called the town clerks to see if they had any records of who fought. Nobody knew, until one elderly town clerk in the southern part of the state said she remembered all the records were sent to the state library in Hartford. I called the state library and they said they had the records, about 5,000 names of Connecticut World War II veterans.

We had to go through the files and pick out those from Iwo Jima. I put a notice in the newspapers that we were going to have a meeting of Iwo Jima survivors at a southern Connecticut American Legion Hall, and we had twenty-four show up from Connecticut. We decided to have another meeting and next time we had thirty-six. We decided to have a formal reunion on February 19, 1988, and we had over one hundred.

This was really a turning point for the Iwo Jima survivors. We were appalled at how many younger people didn't know where Iwo Jima was, what war it was in, what happened there. Some thought it was a Boy Scout troop—Iwo Jima survivors. So at the reunion I got up and said, "I think we should form an organization and set a goal to erect a memorial for the 6,421 men who were killed at Iwo Jima."

They all were in agreement and we formed the Iwo Jima Survivors Association and became incorporated.

We had to raise over a half million dollars, and we didn't request or receive one dollar of local, state, or federal money. We raised all the money ourselves, and we're very proud of this. We stood on street corners, went to fairs, went to malls. We raised money for five years. It was really miraculous.

Some of the people who contributed services were like angels. They came out of nowhere. They weren't survivors of the battle, just people who wanted to help us out. I can't get over it. It is an incredible story.

CHAPTER 6

World War II

Gerhard L. Weinberg

This noted historian's masterful examination of World War II, *A World at Arms: A Global History of World War II,* is a classic. There were many turning points during World War II, the main one being that Germany, Japan, and Italy declared war on the wrong people.

Germany initiated another world war in September 1939. The Italians had launched a colonial war in East Africa in 1935-36, but this was really a resumption of the colonial wars of the late nineteenth century. Similarly, Japan had begun hostilities against China in 1931 and 1937, again a resumption of the kind of war Japan had launched first against China, then against Russia, at the turn of the century.

What Germany started in September 1939 was another world war, when most people thought one per century was plenty. Once it was started by the Germans, the next major turning point comes in August-September 1940, when the Germans are halted by the British in the west and are held to the mainland of the European continent.

The next major turn comes in July and August of 1941 when it becomes clear the Germans are going to lose on the Eastern Front. They attacked the Soviet Union in June 1941, but the critical issue in the long run was not whether this town or that town would fall, or this river or that river be crossed. The critical issue from the beginning was whether the Soviet regime could maintain control of the unoccupied parts of the country and mobilize the human and material resources to defeat the invader.

It should be remembered that in the Second World War the Germans advanced further than in the First World War. The critical difference was that in the First World War the Czarist regime could not keep control of the country, nor could its replacement provisional government.

Napoleon got all the way to Moscow, but the Russian government of Alexander I kept control of the rest of the country and thrashed Napoleon. So the critical issue in 1941 in terms of the outcome of World War II was not this battle or that battle, but whether the Soviet regime of Josef Stalin could, in spite of initial big tactical defeats, maintain control of the country. And by late July, early August it was clear they could do so.

The next major turning point comes in December 1941 when the Japanese decide that fighting China for four and a half years is not enough. They want to take on the Americans, British, and Dutch in perdition. Of course, the German and Italian governments had been encouraging them to do so. The drawing of the United States into the war by Japan, Germany, and Italy is the next major shift.

In 1942 there are a series of actions which channel the war. In early May British forces land on the island of Madagascar in the Indian Ocean and thus secure the Indian Ocean communication route, which was central for the Allies, and made it difficult, if not impossible, for the Axis powers to meet coming from east and west. In June comes the Battle of Midway, in which the Japanese are halted going east.

In July-August come the critical halts to the German offensives into the Middle East that would have shifted the oil resources from the Allied to the Axis side. They're halted in the North by the Russians at Stalingrad and in the Caucuses, and are halted at almost the same time in North Africa by the British at Alamein.

In July 1943, in the Battle of Kursk, the Russians finally and firmly seize the initiative from the Germans, and with some setbacks, head for Central Europe.

In June 1944, critical things occur both in Europe and Asia: the success of the D-Day landing in Normandy, a much riskier operation than most people in retrospect realize, and the success of the Russian offensive on the central part of the Eastern Front. A few days after the D-Day landings are firmed up Russia rips open the German Eastern Front, followed by a series of further dramatic advances, meaning that the Germans will be unable to shift forces back and forth because they're being clobbered in the west and the east, and that is being accentuated by the Allied offensive in Italy at the same time.

In the Pacific in those same summer weeks of June 1944, there is on the one hand a big Japanese victory, and on the other hand a big Japanese defeat. The victory in China by the Japanese destroys the armies of the Chinese Nationalists led by Chiang Kai-shek, and in the long run this opens the road to the communist takeover of China.

At the same time a Japanese offensive into India is crushed by the British-Indian Fourteenth Army, and the Americans are landing in the Mariana Islands, starting with Saipan. The whole subsequent configuration of the war in East Asia is redirected in the summer of 1944.

The major event of 1945 is the fighting on Okinawa in April, May, and June. On land, in the air, and at sea, it is the bloodiest of the battles between the Japanese and Americans and shows that although the Japanese can continue, and do continue to fight exceedingly hard, the Americans can crush the most effective resistance the Japanese forces have put up until that point in the Pacific war.

Then, in early August, the dropping of the atomic bombs provides those in Japan who want to get out of the war a way to do so, as opposed to those who would rather go on fighting in the hope of crushing an American invasion of Kyushu, which they are expecting later that year; therefore, the war ends.

There were those in Germany who tried to end the war in July 1944 after Normandy and the Eastern Front, but they were not successful. That meant the war in Europe would grind down, not wind down, with enormous casualties and destruction, but the outcome was predetermined. The last terrible part of World War II in Europe reveals what the struggle in Japan would have been like if the coup attempt in Tokyo in August '45, by those who wanted to keep on fighting, had succeeded. Fortunately, the coup attempt failed. Unfortunately, the coup attempt in Germany in July 1944 also failed, but both attempts failed very narrowly.

Hitler was on the whole a rather effective leader. It doesn't make sense to demonize him or to suggest that all the errors that were made by his generals should now be retroactively put on his back because they lived to write their memoirs and he didn't. They were all generally in agreement on the major issues and when there were differences of opinion, many of the military agreed with Hitler and some disagreed.

Furthermore, he often disregarded advice that would have been catastrophic for Germany. The commander-in-chief of the German Navy wanted to go to war with the United States in October 1939. Hitler was smart enough to suggest they wait a while.

It makes nice reading and entertaining material to write off people as sort of crazy, but I don't think it gives much insight. On all the major critical issues the people at the top of the German hierarchy were in agreement, and when they were in disagreement it was usually on details; sometimes Hitler was right and sometimes his advisors were right. What was shared by all those at the top in Germany was a complete misjudgment of the Soviet Union and the United States.

There was opposition among the German specialists about going to war with the Soviet Union and practically none about going to war with the United States. This suggests something that is characteristic of the so-called educated elites in Germany, which is an almost unbelievable degree of ignorance about the United States. It was true in the first half of the twentieth century. It was true of the second half of the twentieth century. And unfortunately, it remains true today.

The Japanese military had been divided into various factions and elements during the 1920s and 1930s. One therefore should be very cautious about generalizations here. There is an enormous amount of information on Tojo before he becomes prime minister and his role in taking Japan into war in October, November, December of 1941. And there is much information on Tojo at the end of the war when he tries to commit suicide and is tried [for war crimes].

Where there is very little scholarship to the best of my knowledge is the period to the summer of 1944 when he is in fact running the country and is not only prime minister, but holds several other important cabinet positions simultaneously. What continues to intrigue me is there is so little information about his role and the extent to which he in fact controlled the decision making in 1942, '43, and the first half of '44.

The basic strategy of Japan was grabbing everything as quickly as possible and fighting to hold it in the hope of making a new arrangement in East Asia under which Japan would keep as much as possible by driving up the cost to the Americans, British, and Chinese to the point they would quit. That was the consistent strategy, and Tojo was a devout believer in it. But the extent to which he played a direct role, that's a subject on which I'm afraid we need a good deal more information.

Let me turn to the subject of Hirohito. The scholarship has made it fairly clear that Hirohito was willing to go along with a whole number of things and did not exert a particularly active influence in the early years. That meant he was prepared to go along with the terrible conduct of the Japanese forces in China, but that doesn't mean he directed it—but was prepared to go along. He was prepared to go along with the terrible experimentation that was carried out on human beings. He was prepared to go to war with the United States. He was prepared to seize what they could, make it as difficult as possible, as costly in blood and treasure as possible to take back what they occupied in hopes of making a deal that would leave Japan with a good deal of what they had conquered.

In the spring of 1945, he begins to have some doubts, particularly [about]the failure of the Japanese to win on Okinawa, which was close to home. [That],[c]ombined with the destruction he could see inflicted on Japan by bombing from the Marianas in particular, began to make him doubtful.

Then in the summer his doubts increased, and at the very end he sees in the dropping of atomic bombs a possible way to end the war. So at the very last minute he steps in. But it is correct to state as some recent scholarship has that he was prepared to go along until very late in the war.

Mussolini is a very curious figure who miscalculated colossally in thinking a powerful Germany would reorganize Europe in such a fashion that if Italy were on its side it could assume a larger role in Southeast Europe and North Africa. And while to some extent, especially in North Africa, the Germans were quite prepared to let the Italians do that, I don't think Mussolini ever quite understood that Italy's position would be weakened, rather than strengthened, by aligning with Germany, because in order to maintain domestic consensus, Mussolini at no time built up the kind of military strength that would have given Italy an opportunity to demonstrate her power in warfare.

It is ironic that Mussolini, one of the few twentieth-century leaders who thought of war as a good thing, actually prepared his country less effectively for war than the pre-1915 Italian government that he so despised. The Italian military went into World War II, especially the army, to a very considerable extent with World War I equipment.

As soon as Hitler comes to power, they immediately began a weapons system to fight the French, Poles, and British. They miscalculate the

Russians, so they never build any new weapons systems to fight them. By 1937 the weapon systems for fighting the war in the west are underway, and he gives orders for the development of weapons systems, airplanes, and super battleships for war with the United States.

One is entitled to the opinion that the premise that Germany will conquer the world is looney, but the deductions drawn from this premise in terms of "well, how do we go about doing this?" are logical and coherent. You and I know it all ends in disaster but there is a coherence to the madness.

In the case of Mussolini, he's going to go into all kinds of wars but doesn't make the preparations for them. It is true the German airplane, as they called it, sometimes called the America bomber, sometimes the New York bomber, doesn't get into production, but at least they begin working on it in 1937. Mussolini's going to fight everybody and anybody, but doesn't make preparations. There is a disconnect that is extraordinary, that has colossal implications for the stability of the fascist system.

Because he's allied with Hitler, Mussolini insists on sending large forces to fight on the Eastern Front. People forget that. Tens of thousands of Italians are killed, wounded, and captured on the Eastern Front. That's where some of Italy's bloodiest losses occurred in World War II.

People in Italy, whose sons, brothers, husbands, and fathers are getting killed in places they've never even heard of, wonder. They can understand fighting in Libya, whether they like it or not. Fighting in Ethiopia, whether they like it or not. Those are places Italians have heard about and Italy's supposed to have and so forth. But what on earth are Italian soldiers doing fighting in the Ukraine and the Caucuses?

There is a de-legitimization of the regime at home, which contributes to the fascist system simply falling apart in the summer of 1943. It isn't just that there are defeats in Greece, East Africa, and North Africa, and then when the Allies land on Sicily the whole thing falls apart. There is a process at home which causes trouble, and of course so many Italians didn't like Germans, as so many Germans didn't like Italians. They did not make very good allies.

The major preparations on which Churchill relied when he took over in May 1940 were of course preparations that had been made by Neville Chamberlain's government.

We tend to forget that Churchill did not go to the nearest Five and Ten and buy a bunch of Spitfire and Hurricane fighter planes. These had all been ordered by his predecessor against vehement opposition. What tends to be forgotten in retrospect is that in the last political election in England, in 1935, Chamberlain is attacked by the opposition as a warmonger. Posters show him wearing a gas mask and holding a rifle with a bayonet, and so on.

This was the man who thought England should have an air force. Imagine such an outrageous idea. This was a man who in 1939 pushed through Parliament the first-time-ever peacetime conscription in England over the unanimous vote of the opposition. Practically everyone in England who was opposed to Chamberlain was opposed to him because he was considered a warmonger.

That's not the picture people have today, but that happens to be the way it went. When Churchill becomes prime minister in May 1940, it is the air force built by his predecessor that wins the Battle of Britain. And that may not be unrelated to the fact that at the end of the Battle of Britain, the victor, Air Chief Marshall Sir Hugh Dowding, is canned. It's the only time in World War II that a government cans the victor in a decisive major battle. It's an interesting development.

Chamberlain was a rather cold fish. Had very few personal friends and was not a person who could inspire people to great effort and major sacrifice. Churchill, on the other hand, was an outgoing, ebullient person, enthusiastic, an individual who could enthuse others and who could in clear language and well-articulated phrases arouse and inspire a people to reach beyond themselves and do things, or at least to try things, that seemed impossible.

There's no question that in terms of leadership in crisis, Churchill was incomparably superior as a wartime leader.

Roosevelt had the same ability as Churchill of articulating ideas in ways masses of people could understand, enthusing them and inspiring them with confidence in the face of what was initially a series of terrible defeats. Furthermore, he had an uncanny talent for picking top people. On the civilian side, people who were willing to say "no" to him; on the military side, people who knew what to do and whom he would back up.

The United States is the only country that went through the Second World War with one army chief of staff, one army air force head, and although in early 1942 he changed the commander of the navy from Stark to King, he finished the war with King. He backed his top people, and the only high-level commander he relieved very reluctantly was Stilwell, who just simply couldn't work with the Chinese and had to be recalled.

When things got tough, Roosevelt picked the right people and stuck with them. Patton made a fool of himself, and there was much uproar in the country, and Eisenhower let Marshall and Roosevelt know, "I need to keep him anyway," and Roosevelt took the political guff for it.

The basic strategic concept which he and Secretary of War Stimson, General Marshall, and the other top commanders were in agreement [on] was to invade northwest Europe. If we were going to defeat the Germans, it wasn't going to be by stepping on their toes in the Mediterranean or in the Aegean, but by stabbing them in the heart. If the United States was going to have something to say about post-war Europe, we had to get into the middle of Europe, not to the Island of Rhodes.

I have always been astonished how people think if the Iron Curtain had gone east/west, in other words, if we had liberated Albania and Bulgaria and what else in the Balkans, and the Russians had taken all of Germany, France, Holland, Belgium and been on the Atlantic, we would have been better off afterward. I've never been able to understand that. It always seemed to me that the basic strategy not only made sense from the point of view of logistics, that is to say supply lines, but made sense militarily and politically.

Wars are not fought because countries have military forces, don't know what to do with them one weekend and decide *why don't we fight our neighbors?* There were earlier world wars. The one that probably affected North America the most was the Seven Years War, what we call the French and Indian War, which decided that the British, not the French, would control most of North America. But if one asks what difference does it make, it is that today the English are predominant in Canada and the people of Quebec have to argue as to whether they should allow street signs in French or in English. But there was never any question that the French were going to have to leave Quebec if the British took over.

The Germans had a very different view of the world when they went to war. They were going to take over the globe, and they meant exactly that. All of it. Not just all of Europe, but Africa and the

Western Hemisphere and anything else they could get their hands on. And in those areas there was going to be a massive demographic shift.

To differentiate World War II from previous wars, among those the Germans were expecting to kill was our Miss America of 1994, who is deaf. All handicapped were to be killed. Among those they were going to kill were the two doctors who licked polio, because they were Jewish.

So, people could continue to suffer from the ravages of polio and if it didn't kill them, but just crippled them, then the government would kill them.

No prior wars this country had been in, or other countries had been in, opened up that possibility. The aims of the Germans in taking over the world were fundamentally different from the aims that motivated the people who fought in the Seven Years War, the people who fought in the First World War.

The Second World War, because of the very special aims the Germans had, was really very, very different, and one needs to pay attention to those aims in order to understand both the nature of the conflict and the significance of its outcome.

CHAPTER 7

The Atomic Bomb

Dan Peterson

During World War II, Dan Peterson's aunt was in communications and information with the Women's Army Corps, managing the switchboard at Los Alamos and handling many important telephone calls relative to the development of the atomic bomb.

She died in 1978 from what her family believes were the effects of radiation; her bones began breaking. The doctors told her she had to decide how she wished to spend her remaining years—sitting, standing, or lying down. While making that decision, she died. Not all of the war's casualties were on the battlefield.

Dan Peterson grew up in Evanston, Illinois. After coaching basketball in the United States, he became one of Europe's most successful coaches. He has written numerous books and articles, and lives in Milan, Italy.

The atomic bomb, Hiroshima, and Nagasaki! It all happened so quickly. World War II was almost into its sixth year and predictions were so negative that it almost made you sick to think of it: It would take at least three more years to end the war in the Pacific, and it would cost over one million American lives.

Instead, World War II was over in a matter of days. No invasion of Japan was necessary. The atomic bomb saw to that.

The first time most Americans heard of its existence was on August 6, 1945, just after "The Thin Man" had blown Hiroshima off the face of the earth. Three days later, a second bomb fell on Nagasaki, which also disappeared in seconds. Three days later Japan sued for peace. Two days later, August 14, was V-J Day, and World War II was history. It had taken one week and one day.

While every American was in the dark regarding the development, experimentation, and planned use of the atomic bomb, I was given a sliver of a clue. But I was just nine years old and didn't pick up the signals that were ever so clear.

Had I been just a little older, I might have read the message that was being sent by, of all people, my Aunt Trudy. As it was, I wasn't able to sort it all out until I heard the news about Hiroshima, saw those newsreels of its awesome destruction, and saw that mushroom-shaped cloud that told me this was no ordinary bomb, no ordinary explosion, but was something else altogether.

In that moment I knew I wasn't like other Americans who felt somewhat detached from the whole thing. Why shouldn't they have felt that way? Wasn't this a weapon that was developed by other people? Didn't all of this take place halfway around the world? Why not feel safely removed from all of that, a spectator of hell on earth?

About the only feelings I shared with those people were the ones that revolved around the relief that the war was over and that our servicemen would soon be coming home. I could relate to that, as I had one uncle in Europe, a veteran of D-Day, and two others in the Pacific, one a navy survivor of kamikaze attacks, the other an army survivor of numerous banzai charges.

My Aunt Trudy was the fourth of that family, my mother's brothers and sisters, in the armed forces: She had joined the WACs in 1942. That was the last my Mother heard of her for over eighteen months, which was strange, considering that they were as close as any two sisters have ever been.

Our first indication that Aunt Trudy was into something unusual came when two Secret Service men came to our house to ask a long series of questions about her, when they referred to her as "Sgt. Gertrude McLay." Shortly after this slightly unnerving experience, my mother began to receive mail from Trudy, all heavily censored. This was a second sign: Why is her mail over 50 percent censored when she is stateside and Uncle J.D.'s mail, from Europe, is barely censored at all? These things just did not add up. Or did they add up, but we just couldn't figure it out?

My mother wrote to her brother, my Uncle J.D., to ask him about the heavy censoring. He said it was a mystery to him, but asked if there was a postmark on the envelope. My mother wrote back and told him the letters came from Los Alamos, New Mexico. He came back with the answer that was clue number three, saying, "There is an old munitions dump down there." My mother began putting all of this information together. Her conclusion: Her sister Trude was working on something top secret that involved experimentation in explosives.

What we learned later was that after her enlistment, training, and rapid promotion, she had been screened and cleared for assignment in 1943 to Los Alamos, a priority-one location, where the United States Army, under the command of Gen. Leslie Groves, was developing the atomic bomb and where they would conduct its first test at Alamogordo. This was the Manhattan Project, the single most top secret operation in U.S. military history.

Aunt Trudy had one of the most highly sensitive positions on the base, as she was the telephone switchboard operator, placed there not only because she could handle the mechanical end of the job but also because of her educational background and complete trustworthiness. She handled all incoming and outgoing calls when she was on shift. No one else touched those lines during her hours of duty.

Her work put Aunt Trudy in contact with the most powerful men in the world on a daily basis. A typical call was something like this: "Dr. [Robert] Oppenheimer? One moment, please. President [Franklin Delano] Roosevelt on the line. Go ahead."

Later the president was Harry S Truman, but the procedure never changed. She needed no help to piece together what was happening. It was all clear to her, and she understood that all this was beyond anyone's imagination.

If she had any doubt as to the power and danger of what was going on, that was swept away the day that almost became doomsday for Los Alamos. Canadian scientist Dr. Louis Slotin was conducting experiments when he saw two components were going to collide. He knew that if this happened there would be nuclear fission, and the first atomic explosion in history would reduce Los Alamos and every living thing within it to a fiery ball of atoms in a millionth of a second.

He knew he had to stop this collision but, knowing his subject, he understood that contact with such heavily radioactive material would cost him his life. He never hesitated, using his hands to stop the movement of the components and avoid [their] becoming "colliders."

As soon as he told his colleagues what had happened, they put him in a lead-lined room especially prepared for such an eventuality. He knew this was fatal, as did everyone on the base. Still the command went out: Call President Roosevelt and see what could be done. Aunt Trudy put through the call. His direct order: Call in every top burn specialist in the United States; take every effort to save this man's life. Aunt Trudy then located and called the burn doctors.

The physicians asked for volunteers among the nurses to enter the lead-lined room. One volunteered and would die of radiation exposure along with Slotin. The doctors had no hope for Slotin's life but they hoped to learn something from this ordeal. They were overwhelmed. While ordinary burns burn from the outside, this was the opposite. The blood turned to water and worked its way out. All now understood what would happen when the atomic bomb fell.

Not long after this incident, which shook Aunt Trudy to her soul, she was given her only furlough of the duration and came back home to see her family in Chicago and visit us in suburban Evanston. We were advised that our telephone would be "under surveillance," a sophisticated way of saying our line would be "tapped" during the day of her visit to us. This was my mother's fourth indication that Aunt Trudy was into something big. I understood I was not to use the telephone that day.

It's not hard to imagine the total security that surrounded her furlough. The Army took no chances that she might carry out anything that might compromise the project, either intentionally or otherwise. Their method left nothing to chance. We've all heard the term "strip search." Well, this went beyond that, and then some. Shortly before her departure, she was led to a room where she was stripped to the skin and was *then* body searched!

She then went, in the nude, to another room where she was given duplicates of every single thing she had left behind in the first room: uniform, underwear, hose, shoes, change purse, combs, hair pins, lipstick, makeup, driver's license, identification, keys, fountain pen, and money. She carried most of this in a shoulder bag purse. For some reason this purse caught my mother's attention. It was the first of its kind she had seen. Up until then women carried "clutch" hand purses or "loop" arm bags. My mother's curiosity was heightened with this observation.

Aunt Trudy would later tell us the Secret Service personnel tracked her every step, convinced at least two agents were following her at all times. Never the same two. In relays. Two were on her flight to Chicago, two more would then take over. And so on.

When she came to our house, they had her marked well. Shortly after her arrival there was a phone call. The caller asked for Sergeant McLay. Her answers were, to say the least, cryptic: "Yes. No. Two hours. About 5:30. No. Nothing. No one. Good-bye."

At this point, my Mother decided to see if she could find out what this was about and asked, "What sort of assignment do you have in the WACs, Trude?"

They were seated in the kitchen, having coffee, when this question was put. I was close by, in the dining room, playing with something or other. As a rule, like most nine-year-olds, I never paid attention when adults conversed, but, as with most young boys, anything to do with the military and the war interested me. I turned to hear what my favorite aunt was about to say.

Her answer hit my mother harder than any punch by any heavyweight boxer. She said, "I'm sorry, Lill, I can't tell you that."

I was just a kid but I fully understood that one sister had said to another that the conversation was over. I was as stunned as my mother. I knew how close these two women were; that there were no secrets between them, that this was the all-time sister-to-sister bond.

My mother nodded as she digested Aunt Trudy's answer. Trudy knew she'd hurt my mom, so she tried to soften the blow a little. She asked, "Lillian, just what do you *think* I'm doing?"

My mother, having taken mental notes on all of this for some time, never hesitated. She said, "I think you are working on a terrible, terrible weapon."

My Aunt Trudy, the world's happiest person, the lady that had read *Bambi* to me as a toddler, broke down and cried.

Like any other youngster, I didn't think grown-ups cried. I was disoriented by the whole thing. My mom. My aunt. The army. The war. A weapon. It was all too unreal for me. What in the world was going on? Whatever, these two women quickly recomposed themselves, and before I knew it Aunt Trudy was on her way back to Los Alamos, having left still another clue.

She had to be back because the U.S. Army was ready to test the atomic bomb on open ground for the first time. This came on July 16, 1945, at Alamogordo, in the Tularosa Valley, below New Mexico's Sacramento Mountains. It went off without a hitch, but the biggest sound may not have been the explosion itself, but that of a lot of breath being let out by a lot of scientists who were not at all certain that the world might not come to an end at that moment.

The problem involved the concept of "chain reaction." Would there be a "chain reaction," or would this be an explosion like any other? If there was a "chain reaction" would it stop or would it go on indefinitely? No one could be 100 percent certain of this. Our computers were not ready for this type of solution. They are today, but this was 1945 and computer science was in its infancy.

Here were the greatest scientists in the world, unable to give a clear answer or a scientifically based opinion on this biggest of questions. To resolve the matter, they called in the greatest brain: Albert Einstein. His would be the voice that counted. Everyone at Los Alamos knew full well why he'd been brought in, and all were holding their breath while he pondered his answer, and even after he gave it. His thinking was that there would be no chain reaction, that it would be an explosion like any other, only bigger, and that it would be confined to the limits imposed by its component weight.

In great secrecy the test was conducted. Einstein guessed right, which is why the world is still here today. Shortly after that, the first atomic bombs—there were only two according to reliable sources, as there was not enough material on hand at the time to produce more—were flown, in sections, to Tinian Island, just 1,800 miles south of Japan in the western Pacific Ocean.

At that point highly qualified military men debated where the first of these weapons should fall. That decision—in part based on weather conditions, in part that it involved so little flying time over land, in part because it was not a primary military target and thus had slightly less anti- aircraft protection—went to the port city of Hiroshima.

Col. Paul Tibbetts, Jr., piloted his B-29 Superfortress, the *Enola Gay,* off the long runway on Tinian in the early dawn of August 6, 1945, and headed for his target, Aioi Bridge, in the heart of Japan's eighth largest city. The atomic bomb, just twenty-eight inches around, about the circumference of a basketball, and just ten feet long, but weighing nine thousand pounds, was let go from a height of some 32,000 feet. It detonated 660 yards above ground, and its epicenter was just 300 yards from Aioi Bridge. Four seconds later, 100,000 of Hiroshima's 300,000 people were dead, and the 200,000 thousand survivors were not much better off.

My father, who knew nothing about Aunt Trudy's visit that day in July, was the one who brought the news. Coming home from his shift with the Evanston Police Department, he came in and said, "We dropped the atom bomb on Hiroshima." Not the "atomic bomb." Not the "A-bomb." It was the "atom bomb," as he and so many others would call it in the days that followed.

No one had heard of Hiroshima before that day, but nobody had to tell us it was a Japanese city—it had a Japanese ring to it, rhyming almost perfectly with the name of a Pacific Island of Japan's we knew all too well, Iwo Jima. At the moment my dad told us what had happened, I understood. I looked at my mom, and she had that look that told me that she, too, had put it all together in that fraction of a second. The mystery was no longer a mystery to us.

CHAPTER 8

A Close Thing

Brig. Gen. Henry Muller

The war with Japan ended on September 2, 1945, and with it
World War II. A new era, the Cold War, was about to begin.
Henry Muller, along with approximately 5,000 Americans,
arrived in Japan September 1, 1945, to accept the surrender.

I entered the Army in 1940 as a second lieutenant in the Army
Reserve and received my commission as a result of ROTC training at
UCLA, then the following year was commissioned into the Regular
Army as a second lieutenant. I spent the war in the Pacific, was G-2 of
the Eleventh Airborne Division. G-2 is the officer on a division staff
that's responsible for the collection and dissemination of combat
intelligence on the enemy. I was a lieutenant colonel during that
period.

Our division was first sent to New Guinea, and after intensive training there we went into combat in the Philippines, first on the island
of Leyte, later on the island of Luzon. Our campaign in Luzon ended
in June 1945, and then we were sent to a rest camp in July '45, shortly before the end of the war.

At that point I was called up to the Eighth Army Headquarters,
which was making plans for the invasion of Japan. There were to be
two separate invasions. [The] first was Operation Coronet, the other
Operation Olympic. The first would have come around October or
November, and we were to land on the southern island of Kyushu
and capture enough of the island to build a number of bases that
would support our next operation, the major one against Honshu,
the island on which Tokyo is located.

I had barely arrived at Eighth Army, was just briefing myself on the basics of the plan which had been prepared by MacArthur's headquarters; the Eighth Army was to be one of four armies landing in Japan.

I remember reading with dismay that the medics expected we would have 900,000 casualties and the Japanese 3,000,000 . . . even as a young fellow that was a startling figure. I thought, 900,000 . . . that's nine times what we get to a big game at the Rose Bowl between UCLA and USC, equal to ten times the population of the state of Nevada at that time. When I heard we weren't going to have to invade as a result of the atomic bomb, I was greatly relieved thinking of the lives that would be saved.

The Japanese had a double whammy with two atomic bombs. Then the Soviet Union entering the war meant many of their troops that might otherwise have been deployed home from Manchuria, Korea, and so forth, in defense of the islands, would now be tied up. The Japanese didn't know we only had two atomic bombs at that time. The thought they would lose a city once every few days was just too much for them.

The emperor made his famous speech in which he told them they had to be prepared to bear the unbearable and endure the unendurable. It was about the 20th of August that I was told to take the advance party of the G-2 section of the Eighth Army to Japan. The main body—the full headquarters—would be coming later from Leyte by ship.

As a small group from the Eighth Army representing the various sections, operations, intelligence, personnel, [and] so forth, we moved in as an advance party. As the name suggests, you go in and get things set up so when the main body comes in you're ready to operate. They sent us up to Okinawa by plane and then there was a delay. We learned later that the Japanese had asked for the delay because of the uncertainty of receiving cooperation in the surrender of some of the Japanese military who were diehards.

It wasn't until the morning of the thirty-first that we took off. It was about a four-and-a-half hour trip from Okinawa into Atsugi Air Base which is some twenty miles from Tokyo and Yokohama.

We got in around eight o'clock. They had assembled aircraft on Okinawa that were taking off every three minutes. They had to come in single file because there was only one runway. A plane took off every three minutes and [one] would land every three minutes. Then there would be a quick break so the planes that had come in could unload quickly, then take off to return to Okinawa.

I was one of the first Americans to enter Japan. We were told to stand easy at Atsugi until we had enough force, which meant two or three battalions. They were bringing in the Eleventh Airborne Division and General Swing, division commander, arrived sometime early in the morning.

The Japanese lieutenant general in charge of the Atsugi Air Base reported to him, and General Swing said, "Well, you can be commanding general of the base if you want, but keep the hell out of my way."

The Japanese general had his mission, and said, "I'm here with 30,000 troops around the air base because things are not completely settled yet."

At one end of the air base were a number of kamikaze planes with their propellers removed. But the troops had decided—they were the fanatical troops—they were not going to surrender, and the Japanese lieutenant general said, "Please don't let any troops get on that end of the air base because we might have a firefight and I'm here to prevent that. I have enough troops here that I can take care of it and I will take care of it."

Which he did. He finally forced them to surrender; what method he used I'm not sure.

We were told nobody was going to go anywhere until General MacArthur arrived at two o'clock. He would go first to Yokohama with a battalion of Eleventh Airborne troopers, then we would go in series. The Japanese had sent vehicles, a couple of decent ones for General MacArthur and some of his principal staff. The rest looked like a used car lot, the worst looking vehicles you'd ever seen because I suppose they didn't manufacture [vehicles] during the war.

When General MacArthur's plane arrived at two o'clock, everybody crowded around the stairs that went up to the plane. The door was open. You didn't see a thing. Not a soul came out for what must have been a full minute. Then he appeared in full uniform with the fancy hat and the corncob pipe, looking slowly to the left, then slowly to the right, surveying the whole scene, which some thought was showmanship. On the other hand, how did you expect the American Caesar to arrive?

If it had been me, I'd have probably tripped on the front step and gone all the way down. But he came with great dignity and allowed everybody to take his picture, which was in the Japanese papers that night and following morning, and he looked very dignified. He then came down the stairs and General Swing, the division commander of the Eleventh Airborne Division, greeted him and pointed out the Eleventh Airborne Division Band, who were ready to play the national anthem.

Airborne troopers were on top of one of the old aircraft hangers and had managed to rig up a pole and were perched there with the American flag. The band struck up the *Star Spangled Banner*, and they pulled up the flag, and there wasn't a dry eye in the house, believe me. Very, very dramatic. Then General MacArthur thanked the bandleader and said it was the sweetest music he'd ever heard.

We were then sent by two or three series on a route the Japanese general had asked us to follow, with Japanese drivers and guides. Of course it was their vehicles; we obviously didn't fly any vehicles in with the first aircraft. It was about a twenty-mile trip into Yokohama, and the headquarters would be in The New Grand Hotel, in Yokohama. The trip in was very dramatic; at every intersection there was a company of Japanese infantry troops. We weren't quite sure why. We realized later they were for our protection.

Each of them acted differently. Some would come to ready arms, some would come to present arms, some would do an about-face and turn their backs to us. The Japanese driver explained that that was very courteous.

We saw no one other than soldiers; the entire area had been cleared the whole way to Yokohama with no sign of life.

We were shocked at the amount of destruction. Every factory was burned, most of the houses along the road gone. We came up over this little bridge into a huge plaza in front of the Yokohama Railroad Station, and it was crowded with people waiting their turn to leave. They had apparently been told to get out. They feared the worst—we were going to bayonet the babies, [that] sort of thing. They'd been told awful propaganda.

It was interesting to drive across the cobblestones in this great plaza with our little convoy because everybody—there must have been 10,000 in the plaza—turned their backs and made an opening for us, and the only noise was our vehicles going across the cobblestones. Again the driver assured us that, "Oh, that's very courteous. They're showing you courtesy."

We went to The Grand Hotel where General MacArthur had his quarters and offices. General MacArthur's headquarters was the overall command. They were the people who were dealing with the Japanese and they were the joint Army-Navy command, as well as joint command for the British, French, and so forth. Ours was the Eighth Army, and the Eighth Army was designated as the Army of Occupation of Japan.

It was a tactical army. We had no direct dealings with the Japanese. We were concerned with the occupation, getting enough forces there to make sure the occupation orders were obeyed and there was no insurrection or disobedience regarding the documents of surrender.

I was the acting G-2 of the Army of Occupation. Sounds pretty important, but at that time we only had one division on shore. I didn't have anything to do and felt funny. I realized G-2 was responsible for combat intelligence of the enemy, but we no longer had any combat, there was no war, we no longer had an enemy. They'd all surrendered. The only thing we could report would be any cases of violence or failure to comply with the occupation orders, but there weren't any. I realized the war had ended, I had done myself out of a job. Of course, we did have things to do later.

The Japanese surrendered as hard as they fought. I believe the first night one Japanese came out in front of the hotel and put a grenade to his chest and killed himself as a protest. It wasn't against us. It was just a protest. He didn't like the idea the Japanese had surrendered, I guess. That was the only act of violence. They were doing their best to cooperate and help our troops move into the positions they were assigned.

No other country could have done what they did without absolute faith and confidence in the divinity and authority of their emperor. The emperor had never, to the best of my knowledge, addressed the Japanese nation on radio. When he went on the radio and explained what was happening, that it was in the best interests of the country to surrender, he finished by saying, ". . . bear the unbearable and endure the unendurable." The Japanese people accepted it, and so did the army for the most part.

It was a tremendous gamble. We didn't know much about their problems with certain army leaders who wished to continue to fight.

The Japanese didn't tell us how difficult the situation was. I don't know how much MacArthur knew about the extent of the resistance. He must have known there was some because he made up his mind to move quickly and took, as he said, "the greatest risk in history and succeeded." If it had failed it would have been a disaster. But he decided the thing to do was to move in fast.

When we found out about the kamikaze troops outside the airport, the Eighth Army commander wired MacArthur, saying perhaps he had better delay this a day until we see what the situation was.

But MacArthur said, "No, I'm coming on in."

If he had delayed, and the kamikaze troops taken credit for having delayed him, that might have given impetus and strength to the recalcitrant units. But he came and it was a *fait accompli.*

Never in history has a conquering force been so overwhelmingly outnumbered as you were. You were all taking your lives in your hands.

Oh, absolutely. Starting with MacArthur, down to the last private that came in that day. I think we had five battalions by the end of the day, possibly four thousand troops, plus another thousand administrators and supply people and so forth. The marines landed the next day at Yokosuka, but that was down at the mouth of Tokyo Bay, where there was a huge Japanese naval base. They only had a few marine units, and we were not in supporting distance of each other. The Japanese had fifteen divisions outside of Tokyo and good Lord knows how many people all over Japan under arms. Certainly between one to two million people against our five thousand.

On September 2nd we had everything prepared for the surrender aboard the *Missouri.* There was a little unhappiness between MacArthur's headquarters and Admiral Nimitz' headquarters regarding MacArthur accepting the surrender. That was Mr. Truman's decision, which meant the Army was going to occupy under General MacArthur.

I can see where Admiral Nimitz, who had fought the war all through the Central Pacific and defeated the Japanese fleet, which was absolutely essential before we could have moved in, might have felt slighted. Mr. Truman settled that by having it aboard the *Missouri,* in Tokyo Bay, just off Yokohama. Admiral Nimitz was standing right behind MacArthur and was accorded the courtesies.

I was much too junior as a lieutenant colonel to get anywhere near the *Missouri.* The pier was carefully guarded and nobody was allowed on except the American and Japanese delegates. But it was guarded by the Eleventh Airborne, and since I'd spent the war with the Eleventh Airborne, I think I still had the patch on, one of their lieutenants came up and said, "Oh, I know you. You're the G-2 of Eleventh Airborne Division. But I don't have authority to let you on."

I said, "I'm not G-2 of Eleventh Airborne Division anymore, I'm G-2 of the whole friggin' army of occupation."

"Oh, oh," he said, "well, okay!"

In any case, I got up on some stairs going up to a warehouse on the pier where I could get a good view and watch the Japanese delegation. That was quite a sight, the members from the foreign office with top hats and stripped coats, then the generals and admirals. You looked at these people and you thought, *this is the first time in centuries Japan had been occupied.*

Here were these Japanese generals who were in command of Japanese troops spread out from Singapore, Indonesia, China, Vietnam, Korea, Manchuria. They must have had 3,000,000 overseas at least, and now the commanding generals were surrendering. This was a very melancholy group.

After the surrender, the next unit in was the First Cavalry. Then one by one all the various divisions came in, commonwealth forces too. Right after the surrender we were told by MacArthur's headquarters to pick up the first ten names on the black list, a list that had been prepared by MacArthur's headquarters of those who were probably responsible for war crimes, or suspected of them.

The first one picked up was Hideki Tojo, former premier, who attempted hara-kari and failed, and lived to be hung later. Also on the list was General Homa, the commanding general of the Sixteenth Division, responsible for the death march on Bataan; they picked him up and he was subsequently hung. In the middle of the list was a name that sounded like a female—Eva D'Aquina.

I said, "Who's that?"

They said, "This is Tokyo Rose."

Her real name was Eva Toguri but she'd married a Portuguese named D'Aquina. This is quite important because being married to a Portuguese she'd accepted Portuguese citizenship, and that meant she wasn't guilty of treason. She was a Portuguese when she did the propaganda broadcasting for Japan.

The CIC [Counter Intelligence Corps] people wanted to bring their prize by so we could see her. They brought her by on some pretext, and when she came into my office I recognized her at once and she recognized me. We'd been classmates at UCLA.

She said, "Henry."

And I said, "Eva, you're not Tokyo Rose?"

"Oh, no, no, no," she said. "It's all a mistake. You'll find out it's all a mistake."

Well, it wasn't a mistake. She was Tokyo Rose. There had been an earlier one, but she was the principal Tokyo Rose.

That's all I saw of her. They rushed her off to jail, but she was acquitted because she was a Portuguese citizen. Also, there was a State Department paper issued during the war stating that anyone who accepted one day's work for the German or Japanese government automatically lost their citizenship. Therefore by our own rules she wasn't a citizen.

Later she was taken back to the United States and tried on some charge. It was a ridiculous charge, and she received a very short prison term, less than a year, something like that. The last I heard she was running a cleaning establishment in Chicago.

Our job was to establish a constitutional government, and it was a complete success. Good Lord, years later we joked we'd done a little bit too well. They were competing with us. All you saw was Japanese cars and radios, and they seemed to be prospering and we were spending huge sums fighting wars. They had gotten rid of their army, and we made them put in their constitution they could not have any military force outside their country.

I'll tell you, that first day is engraved in my memory, the moment I saw the flag go up in Japan and heard the National Anthem played, that was the day I knew the war was over, more important than the 2nd of September.

CHAPTER 9

FDR and Pearl Harbor

Robert B. Stinnett

There was no more galvanizing event for Americans in the twentieth century than the Japanese sneak attack on Pearl Harbor. Up until 7:53 A.M. Hawaiian time, on December 7, 1941, most Americans were isolationists. At 9:35 A.M. the Japanese attack ended with 2,273 army and navy dead, 1,119 wounded. Sixteen warships out of 101 in anchorage incurred major damage. The *Utah, Oklahoma, Arizona, Cassin* and *Downes* were all knocked out of World War II. A total of 188 army, navy, and marine planes were lost. Isolationism ended.

From 1982 to the present, Robert Stinnett has researched the attack. With interviews, investigation, and documents now available through the Freedom of Information Act he has shown in his book *Days of Deceit* that not only FDR, but other government officials knew the attack was coming. Their rationale apparently was that Pearl Harbor was a small price to pay to unify the country for war.

There is a memorandum that Lt. Cmdr. Arthur H. McCollum wrote to his boss, Capt. Walter S. Anderson, the director of naval intelligence (McCollum was head of the Far East desk of the Office of Naval Intelligence). It was delivered October 6, 1940, and McCollum outlined the military problems facing the United States at that time from Adolf Hitler.

The idea was to overcome the isolation movement in this country which was intent on keeping the U.S. out of the European war. McCollum advocated directing eight actions at Japan that would cause them to commit an overt act of war against the United States, and thus bring themselves, Germany, and Italy into war against us.

[Editor's Note] The eight actions McCollum predicted that would lead to a Japanese attack on the United States were:

   A. *Make an arrangement with Britain for the use of British bases in the Pacific, particularly Singapore.*

   B. *Make an arrangement with Holland for the use of base facilities and the acquisition of supplies in the Dutch East Indies—now Indonesia.*

   C. *Give all possible aid to the Chinese government of Chiang Kai-shek.*

   D. *Send a division of long-range heavy cruisers to the Orient, Philippines, or Singapore.*

   E. *Send two divisions of submarines to the Orient.*

   F. *Keep the main strength of the U.S. Fleet, now in the Pacific, in the vicinity of the Hawaiian Islands.*

   G. *Insist that the Dutch refuse to grant Japanese demands for undue economic concessions, particularly oil.*

   H. *Completely embargo all trade with Japan, in conjunction with a similar embargo imposed by the British Empire.*

All eight actions were important, but the most important was Action F, keeping the fleet at Pearl Harbor as an enticement or a lure to Japan to attack. FDR adopted every one of the actions, so obviously he knew about them.

There were twenty-five Pacific Rim listening posts in the Pacific Basin. Most were run by the United States, and the others were operated by England, Canada, and the Dutch. Adm. Harold Stark was President Roosevelt's chief of naval operations. It was Stark who called this "a splendid arrangement," meaning these twenty-five monitoring stations that were listening in on Japanese military and diplomatic message interceptions. These listening posts were in place by September 1941 and were up and running.

Adm. Husband E. Kimmel, commander in chief, Pacific Fleet, received information the Japanese submarine fleet was heading toward Hawaii. Naval planning taught that if you find submarines, then look for carriers. Kimmel was worried about that and tried to get Washington to unleash him, take the handcuffs off of him. But

Washington did not want that because they wanted an overt act of war.

The North Pacific was declared a vacant sea on November 25, 1941, and all United States and Allied shipping was prohibited from this area. This was the same day the Japanese carrier force sortied into the North Pacific and proceeded to Pearl Harbor. This was known by the commandants of the Twelfth Naval District in San Francisco because they controlled the shipping.

On Sunday, November 23, Admiral Kimmel had the Pacific Fleet in the exact spot where Japan would launch against Pearl Harbor two weeks later, on December 7. He had the fleet there looking for a "Japanese carrier force." He called it an exercise, but once Washington learned he had the fleet there, they ordered it out. Therefore, Admiral Kimmel cancelled the exercise and brought the ships back to Pearl Harbor, and that's where most of them remained.

Located north of Hawaii are a number of underground volcanos called the Classical Composer Seamounts, and one of them is the Prokofiev Seamount. That is where Japan launched the Hawaii attack, and where Admiral Kimmel two weeks earlier had the Pacific Fleet.

Since the United States was intercepting the Japanese foreign ministry radio messages, they knew Tadashi Morimura was assigned to the Japanese Consulate at Honolulu. But he was not on the Japanese foreign ministry diplomatic list, so that caused immediate consternation; that was very unusual. He was also twenty-nine years old and Japan rarely sent young people to Hawaii because that was an ideal place to go prior to your retirement.

His real name was Takeo Yoshikawa and he was a Japanese naval ensign. He arrived March 26, 1941, and the White House and FBI knew he was arriving, prepared for him, and watched his actions. Once he arrived, he immediately obtained a census of the U.S. Pacific Fleet, where the warships went on maneuvers, all the details on how they and the Army and Air Force were operating in the Hawaiian area. We were intercepting his messages and all this information went to Roosevelt.

Beginning August 1941, the spy began establishing grid coordinates for Pearl Harbor so Tokyo could prepare maps of anchorages for the torpedo pilots of the First Air Fleet.

President Roosevelt ordered the Panama Canal closed to Japanese shipping in July 1941 which forced Japan to send their ships down around Cape Horn—around the Strait of Magellan. It was another harassment of Japan, followed shortly by a total embargo of Japan which then set Japan on the course of war. This was Commander McCollum's Action H, which was the total embargo of Japan. President Roosevelt signed that. It was an executive order, and a direct link to McCollum.

On November 27 an order came from Admiral Stark sending two carrier task forces totaling about twenty-five ships out of Pearl Harbor to deliver airplanes to Wake Island and Midway Island. The carriers were the *Enterprise* and the *Lexington,* along with support vessels of cruisers and destroyers, the most modern ships in the Pacific Fleet. Airplanes were delivered to Wake, [but] none were delivered to Midway.

This left mostly old warships in Pearl Harbor, relics of World War I. There were battleships, about six cruisers which were fairly modern, and some destroyers there mainly for upkeep.

The carriers and support vessels were in the Central Pacific, [while] the Japanese carrier force was in the North Pacific. The American carrier force was sent in the path of the oncoming Japanese submarine fleet. It has never been explained. The Japanese carrier force was roughly forty degrees north latitude and the submarine force was twenty degrees North latitude. Midway is about twenty-five degrees north latitude.

It doesn't make any sense unless they were trying to get the Japanese to attack these two carrier forces, but apparently neither one saw the other. I'm not convinced that that didn't happen, because there were approximately thirty Japanese submarines proceeding east toward the Hawaiian Islands.

General Marshall, as well as President Roosevelt, was reading the Japanese Naval dispatches Saturday, November 15, 1941. At that time General Marshall called the Washington bureau chiefs of the major news media to his office in the War Department Building. He pledged them to secrecy, which they all agreed to, then alluded they'd broken the Japanese code, were reading their messages, and predicted war would break out within the first ten days of December.

On November 5, the chief of the naval general staff of Japan sent a message to the combined fleet of Japan stating that war would start the first week of December against the United States, Britain, and the Netherlands. So Marshall had to receive his information from that message.

And that message was intercepted in Hawaii on November 5 by Station H, and the one who confirms it is Lt. Cmdr. Joseph J. Rochefort, commander, Station HYPO, Pearl Harbor. He told Admiral Kimmel that he'd intercepted a message from the chief of the naval general staff of Japan on November 5, but did not say what the contents were. He issued a daily communications intelligence summary, and that's how we know he intercepted the message.

Rochefort's organization intercepted the messages and provided information to Kimmel's intelligence officer, Lt. Cmdr. Edwin Layton. Rarely did Rochefort deliver it directly to Kimmel. It went through Layton, though we have instances where Admiral Kimmel bypassed Layton and went directly to Rochefort's headquarters to seek information, indicating Kimmel was suspicious of Layton, didn't trust him, and bypassed him when he wanted accurate information.

From the day the Japanese carrier force departed the Kurile Islands, the admiral in charge, Adm. Chuichi Nagumo, was in extensive radio communications with the submarine fleet commander and also the Central Pacific commander. This is according to Rochefort's daily summary that he sent to Kimmel. But none of these have been released yet, though we know from each message number how many are missing since each message was numbered by the Japanese. Over 90 percent of the messages that were sent are still in the censor's files in the United States.

More and more records are being released. There are millions of records that we have to go through. They're not indexed, they're scattered, they've been dispersed, but there is a big file of them at Archives Two in College Park, Maryland, and hopefully we're going to find them.

Vice Admiral Inoue was the commander of Japan's Fourth Fleet in the Central Pacific. He was in charge of invading and seizing Wake Island and Guam, as well as supporting the Japanese submarine fleet. He alerted his command [that] war was to start on December 8, Tokyo time.

On December 2, Tokyo time, Admiral Yamamoto, the operations chief of the Japanese Navy, met with Emperor Hirohito and was given an Imperial command to begin the war on December 8, Tokyo time. At that time Admiral Yamamoto sent out the code: *CLIMB MOUNT NIITAKA, 1208 REPEAT 1208*. That was the signal to start the war, and it was intercepted in Hawaii at the time of transmission, December 1, Hawaii time.

Commander Layton said it was never transmitted—he has about six or seven different versions. But the person who intercepted that message is still alive and lives in Kent, Washington, and he confirmed that he intercepted the message. His name is Joseph Howard.

There was plenty of military information on what was going to happen. Also there were intercepts involving the German ambassador and Tokyo that warned war was going to break out suddenly in the next few days. These were diplomatic messages, and read with the military messages, specifically said Pearl Harbor.

Roosevelt certainly knew they were going to be attacked after the carrier task force departed the Kurile Islands. That is when he personally authorized the order to the Pacific commands to stand aside and let Japan commit the first overt act. That is right out of McCollum's memo when he said, "Don't go on the offense. Keep your defenses up, but don't be offensive. No offensive operations." In other words, don't go out looking for them.

As far as is known, Kimmel and Lt. Gen. Walter Short, Hawaii's army commander, received none of the information which showed the carrier force was coming. Basically, both were told to stand aside and let Japan commit the first overt act of war. They followed orders and did not have their reconnaissance up and running.

It was quite well understood that Japan was to commit the first overt act of war, and Commander Rochefort is quoted as saying that it was a cheap price to pay to unify the country. This is what most naval officers felt at the time, that we were in deadly peril from Adolf Hitler and if we didn't wake America up, there was a strong chance we would be defeated.

Admiral Kimmel knew thirty Japanese submarines were heading toward or at least were heading in an easterly direction toward Hawaii, including not only the submarines but their commander and all their support ships—oilers and that sort of thing. He knew they meant business, but he had to take orders from the commander in chief and stand aside and let Japan commit the first overt act of war.

In May 2000, I spent a week at the National Archives and discovered more information on the Japanese encoded messages. It is just astounding. We were tracking all the carriers and Admiral Nagumo, the commander of the carriers. We knew when he formed his carrier task force and his association with the tankers that were going to accompany him on this long journey across the North Pacific to refuel his force.

It takes a strong commander to make this type of decision and that's what Roosevelt was, a strong commander. The safety of the few can be discarded, you might say, for the benefit of the many. There was no other option for him. I've given many talks before military and historical groups and this is one of the things that is discussed: Were there other options? I don't see it.

The only option he had was to create an outrage on the American public, and Japan attacking us at Pearl Harbor created the outrage. That was the strategy, and it worked. The next day the country was totally unified.

Commander McCollum wanted a clean-cut, overt act of war. If we'd intercepted their ships in the North Pacific, the isolationists would have said we provoked them or that we had a chip on our shoulder. McCollum wanted a clean-cut, overt act of war.

Immediately after, Kimmel and Short were relieved of duty. Walter Short kept his lieutenant general's commission, but Husband Kimmel was broken from a four-star admiral to rear admiral, a two-star rank. They couldn't say much, because it would reveal we had broken the Japanese naval codes, and during wartime we certainly didn't want that known.

General Short died of a broken heart in 1947. He had heart trouble right after he was relieved and, according to his family, that was the cause of death. Admiral Kimmel lived until 1968. He tried to fight it, but all the information that exonerates him was withheld from him, and was not given to the joint congressional committee that investigated the disaster in 1945-46, nor was it given to the 1995 investigation.

There are two smoking guns. McCollum's eight-action memo and the breaking of radio silence by the Japanese on their way to Hawaii—and our intercepting, decoding, and translating these key messages—knowing they were coming.

CHAPTER 10

Harry S Truman

David McCullough

Harry Truman took office April 12, 1945, within hours of FDR's death. Roosevelt had not confided in him. Therefore Truman came to the presidency poorly prepared during one of history's most dangerous times. Truman met the test with vitality, courage, determination, and character, assuring him a place as one of our great presidents.

David McCullough won the Pulitzer Prize for *Truman*, his major biography of Harry S Truman.

No president in our history, including Franklin Roosevelt and Abraham Lincoln, ever had to face decisions that were so momentous and so far reaching in such a short time. The fact that he was able to withstand the pressure, emotional and physical, as well as mental, is a sign of what sort of stuff he was made of. It's also a sign of the quality of people he had around him.

He had several disadvantages. It wasn't just that Roosevelt had told him nothing about the atomic bomb, Roosevelt had told him nothing about anything. He was privy to no inside information, or any expertise from advisors. A president normally takes office having won an election, having run for office, having chosen certain people to guide him who were expert in economics or military affairs or foreign policy or whatever.

Truman had no such coterie. He had no friends in the foreign policy establishment. He counted no economists, military historians, or scholars among his friends and associates. So when he stepped into office, he's stepping in cold, not just in what he knows, but as far as who's with him.

The people who are with him, of course, are Roosevelt's own people. By and large they were extremely able and, of course, they were richly experienced because of the intensity of the previous several years during the war. People like [George] Marshall, Admiral King, Admiral Leahy, Harry Hopkins—who was very ill, but nonetheless still there—were the people advising him. He didn't know Secretary of State Stettinius, for example. They may have said "hello" on occasion, but he didn't know him.

He knew nothing about our policy toward the Soviet Union. What we were intending for the very difficult months ahead in peacetime. It was one of the reasons he'd never wanted to be nominated as vice-president; and become president. It wasn't that he didn't want to become president; he didn't want to become president after Franklin Roosevelt. He had this huge shadow of the great man hanging over him. He knows whatever he does he's not going to be judged according to whether he did the right or wrong things, or the best thing for the country, or the best thing for the world, or the moral or immoral thing or whatever, he's going to be judged against Franklin Roosevelt. No matter what he does.

That was a burden very few presidents have ever had to carry. President Johnson, I suppose, in the wake of the death of Abraham Lincoln would be the closest to it.

Truman is coming in in the wake of a world calamity. The most important event of the century. And 1945 is not just the most important year of the century, it's one of the most important years of all time; the trauma of Roosevelt's death, the trauma of the end of the war, and the fact that human beings are forced to look into the pit of evil as never before. At Hiroshima and Nagasaki, but also at Dachau and Buchenwald, and the horrible realization that all the rumors and reports coming out of Germany of the Holocaust were true and worse than anyone realized.

It would have been a very difficult time for anyone who had spent years in preparation for the job. But he stood up, and he measured up. He is the classic example of the seemingly ordinary person, who faced with extraordinarily difficult circumstances, rises to the occasion and performs in an extraordinary way, which is a great American theme.

Stalin is not a figment of the imagination. Many Cold War historians treat the Soviet Union as that *National Geographic* phenomenon on the other side of the world. Stalin was a real person and a real embodiment of evil. We knew it, and knew it increasingly as time went on. In hindsight, we know him to have been one of the monstrous human beings of all-time. Perhaps a more evil force than even Hitler.

Nobody read Stalin well, not even Churchill. Joseph Stalin was a consummate, brilliant actor. He fooled them all, including Truman. Truman had this traditional and rather naive American idea that we can sum people up by just looking them in the eye. You meet a fellow face-to-face, you know the stuff he's made of, etc. Truman couldn't have been more wrong. He said, "Joe Stalin was as near to Tom Pendergast as any man I ever met." Well, he was nothing like Tom Pendergast.

Truman is ignoring Soviet, Russian history, the whole culture and firestorm of life in Russia in the twentieth century. He has no conception of what kind of human being that might have produced. He stated privately in one of his letters or journals, "I was mistaken and naive and didn't understand."

On June 25, 1950, the North Koreans invaded South Korea and we responded. The war dragged on for three years. Truman thought his conduct of this war was his greatest contribution as president. This is ironic since the Korean War brought down his presidency.

Yes, but you see he was willing to sacrifice his own political hide for what he thought was right. There's a line in my book [*Truman*] when Sam Rosenman was asked at one point, "What was the greatest difference between Truman and Roosevelt?" Rosenman, having worked for Roosevelt, too, said, "Oh, it was that Truman seemed much less concerned, often seemed not concerned at all, about how his decisions would affect his own political fortunes." The Korean War is a far more interesting, and far more important event in our history than we have so far recognized.

Truman felt the decision to go into the Korean War was the most difficult decision of his presidency. That's very interesting historically, but it's also very interesting in understanding Truman. Most people have no idea today, and if they ever did know it, have long forgotten. It was the most popular decision he ever made. When Truman announced we were sending support for the South Koreans, who were being overrun by the invasion from the North, the country gave its virtual unanimous approval, and there was unity of approval on Capitol Hill, with only a few exceptions.

It was as if finally, finally he's acting like an American president. It's only a few months later when the war goes so terribly sour, when it looks like we're going to have our own Dunkirk in Korea, that it becomes Truman's war.

I think the fact that he didn't use atomic bombs in Korea is an aspect of his presidency, a high mark of his presidency, for which he's been given far too little credit. We can't just judge presidents by what they do. We also have to judge them by what they don't do. The fact that President Eisenhower didn't go into Vietnam is a very important credit to his administration. The fact that there was no missile gap during the Eisenhower years as charged by the Democrats when they ran against him in 1960 is greatly to Eisenhower's credit.

Truman didn't use atomic bombs, as MacArthur wanted, against China to resolve the Korean War. The fact that he was ready to settle for a stalemate to avoid nuclear world war is immensely to Truman's credit in my view, and one of the most important decisions of his presidency. He knew that history would judge him to have done the right thing in the long run. The reason that Harry Truman stands the test of time, increasingly stands the test of time, is that he understood because of his sense of history that the test of time is the one that matters, the one that counts.

It's why he can rise out the abuse that he's subjected to after firing MacArthur. He knew this was a response of the moment and that the thing that counted was how the country and history would judge him in the long run.

MacArthur's firing was very dramatic. In lecturing around the country at colleges and universities, I've tried to emphasize what a moment this was. I believe if George Bush had fired General Schwarzkopf in the midst of the Gulf War it would have been rather mild compared to what it was to wake up and hear Harry Truman had fired General MacArthur.

He's so often criticized for making snap judgments. These shoot-from-the-hip decisions—and if you examine the record, if you look at what was going on and who was telling him to get rid of MacArthur—the conclusion you come to is it's a wonder he didn't do it sooner.

I think one of the most telling moments of all is when John Foster

Dulles, who was the foreign policy spokesman for the opposition party, returns from a trip to the Far East and seeing MacArthur early in the Korean War says, "You better get rid of him quickly. He's going to be trouble. He's over the hill."

There were scandals in his administration. Shabby stuff. I don't know, it's a flaw.

He did move about as quickly as he could on the IRS scandals cleaning out those people. But it was very hard for him to accept that people he liked, people he'd known for a long time, might be corrupt. He was too quick to say, "Well, that's just what my opponents are claiming."

But we've seen that so often since. So much of what he was being criticized for, by today's standards at least, seems very tame. Very tame. But that is not to excuse it. It was shabby. It was in part, and I think he knew this, that his party had been in power too long. I think he really understood it was perhaps time for a different regime to come in.

I think one of the things about the fifties that people forget, particularly Hollywood when the fifties are recalled and recreated in films, is how scary it was. The idea that we faced annihilation, that we faced the prospect of atomic war. President Eisenhower evacuating the White House to go to a secure place. Reading headlines when you're in high school that we're going to proceed with the hydrogen bomb. It was scary!

For example, the idea that the 1920s was all bathtub gin and raccoon coats and Stuts Bearcats is a misconception. There are many misconceptions about the 1950s that are equally erroneous and unfair. It was a much more interesting time than is generally portrayed and a time of immense importance.

Truman had one of the most eventful presidencies in our history—the Marshall Plan, the Truman Doctrine, NATO, the Berlin Airlift, the recognition of Israel. The first president ever to send a civil rights message to congress. The desegregation of the armed forces. The creation of the Defense Department as we know it and a secretary of defense. The creation of the CIA. The National Security Council. The creation of the Atomic Energy Commission under civilian control. The decision to go ahead with the hydrogen bomb. The decision to go into Korea. The decision to fire MacArthur. The decision not to use atomic bombs in Korea.

This is a staggering presidency in the momentous nature of the decisions and the courage it took to proceed with many of those decisions.

But even with that, the most important aspect of Truman's presidency in hindsight is Truman himself. The kind of person he was. Particularly in view of what has become of the presidency since. The influence of publicity, public relations, "spin doctors," overnight polls, and talk show influence and all of that.

Here was a man without artifice, who didn't fake, who didn't fudge, who didn't whine, didn't lie, knew who he was, tried as best he could at everything he had to do, meant what he said and said what he meant, and who tried above all to do what was best for the country. As he became fully cognizant of the horror science had introduced into warfare, [he] tried to do what was best for the world.

He had enormous courage. He had remarkable civility. He was very much more than "give 'em hell, Harry." Very much more than plain-speaking, down-home, salty Missouri Harry.

He had great native intelligence, great common sense. He believed in this country, believed in the system to his boots. Now he wasn't perfect by any means. He made some big mistakes. His loyalty oath program was a terrible thing; it was costly in five or six ways. His appointments weren't always the best. His Supreme Court appointments were not particularly distinguished. The appointment of Louis Johnson to secretary of defense was as bad a decision as he made.

He should have fired J. Edgar Hoover. He never had cause to, and therefore decided he couldn't, but he certainly would have liked to have done it. The seizure of the steel industry in the last part of his administration was high-handed and rightly judged unconstitutional. He was intemperate at times in what he said and what he wrote. He was a very human man.

But in many ways he's an allegorical figure. He's Harry "True-Man," from a place called Independence. So much of what he had been through in life was a representation of what the country had been through, that in many ways he was among the best-prepared presidents we've ever had. So that while he didn't know about foreign policy and he didn't know about the atomic bomb, and he didn't have influential or brilliant friends or friends whose expertise would benefit him when he first took office, he had a background in American life that was not only authentic, but potent. And gave him a kind of vitality and confidence that would see him through terrible times.

My favorite explanation of Truman's essential character is [Dean] Acheson's comments, which are in his book *President at the Creation*, which I quote in my book. He uses the lines from Shakespeare's *Henry V* when King Henry—King Harry—goes among the troops, the frightened, dispirited troops in the dark, in the night before the Battle of Agincourt and says,

> . . . every wretch pining and pale before,
> Beholding him, plucks comfort from his looks . . .
> His liberal eye doth give to every one . . .
> A little touch of Harry in the night.

And that's what he did. When things looked their bleakest, that's when he wasn't just at his best, but he was often at his most cheerful and his most confident. He understood that you cannot lead by just telling people what they want to hear.

When he's told, "If you persist with your civil rights program, you're going to lose the 1948 election," he says, "If I lose because of that, I will have lost for a good cause."

How wonderful! How wonderful! When he's told by Bob Hannegan, "Look, if you try and go ahead and reorganize the Defense Department, you're going to lose. You're up against this entrenched old system, and they're going to knock your block off. You're going to lose. Furthermore, even if you win, you're going to gain no political mileage out of it. You're going to do nothing for yourself politically."

And he says, "I'm going to do it because it needs to be done."

Now that's a real guy.

I think he was the greatest human being we've had in the White House this past century. I think the greatest president of that century will probably, in the long run, have to be judged. I will have to say it was Roosevelt, because he saw us through the two worst crises of the century: the Great Depression and the Second World War. From 1933 to 1945 is only twelve years. But Truman is my *favorite* president. I like him because he's such a great story.

I like Truman because he's one of us. If he could do it, by God, we can do it. If he can be that way, why can't we all be that way? He was without privilege, without advantage. He walks on stage and he's five feet,nine inches, and he has a strong, to many people, nasal Missouri twang, and he isn't handsome, and he has thick glasses. But he's the real thing.

CHAPTER 11

A Fortunate Succession

Robert H. Ferrell

This renowned Truman historian and biographer has written and edited eleven books on the thirty-third president. He is certain the nation and the world would have experienced a far different post-war period if Henry Wallace had remained Roosevelt's vice presidential running mate in 1944. Instead, FDR chose Harry Truman, and the free world benefitted greatly.

In the history of the American presidency, it seems clear that the most awkward succession, one president to another, occurred on April 12, 1945, when Franklin D. Roosevelt died and his successor became Harry S Truman. The result, surely, was marvelous: Truman made a first-rate president. But the way in which it occurred was involuted, to a point where events easily could have gone in other ways.

During the initial months of 1944, when Roosevelt should have been making up his mind as to whom he would select as his vice presidential running mate, he did not appear to be giving the matter much, if any thought. This was in part because none of his vice presidents had seemed important to him. He gave little attention to his first vice president, John Garner, who was reelected in 1936. Garner was not close to Roosevelt, and by 1940 had become virtually estranged—for Garner wanted the 1940 Democratic nomination for the presidency and Roosevelt instead desired a third term. FDR then turned to Henry A. Wallace, and again there was distance, something close to estrangement.

The Wallace vice presidency, 1941-45, is of much interest. Wallace was not a political man, and this was one of the reasons Roosevelt did not find him interesting. What I find of interest in 1944 is that FDR would have taken Wallace for a second vice presidential term. It would have been an extraordinary situation if Wallace had become president. The only time he ran for public office was in 1940 for the vicepresidency. He would have been a risky president. I've often thought how fortunate it was that Truman, rather than Wallace, became president in 1945.

Wallace said he was interested in issues, not people. Now . . . no political leader can say such a thing. Politics is personal. It's knowledge of people. Wallace was an austere man. He would not have made a good political leader. Furthermore, he was innocent concerning the Soviet Union. Many people were innocent at that time, but he was more innocent than most.

James Byrnes desired the vice presidency in 1944, and would have made a better president than Wallace, but he too suffered from defects. At that time, he was Roosevelt's principal administrative assistant in the White House. He had been senator from South Carolina for many years, and occupied a seat on the Supreme Court for a year, and FDR then had brought him into the executive offices to assist in administrative tasks during the war.

He was a Southerner and perhaps too proud of it, and by later standards, a racist. He felt that the arrangements in the South whereby blacks were ineffective politically were all right. He was too proud, saw slights rather easily, felt that Mr. Roosevelt was not paying sufficient attention to him after Mr. Roosevelt described him as his "assistant president." He was constantly threatening to resign. He was not as stable a person, and I think the presidency would have demanded too much of him; he would not have been a good president.

There was a White House meeting just before the Chicago convention in 1944 and FDR came out for Truman. After that he told Wallace and Byrnes that each could go ahead and try for the vicepresidency. Roosevelt was not sure what he should do, and behind that lay the fact he didn't much care; he didn't consider the office important.

Truman's nomination was managed by the party bosses, a group of half a dozen men. One was Edwin Pauley, the national committee's treasurer, a very important position. Pauley was a California oilman and a direct and forceful person, not a Wallace enthusiast. One could almost say he hated Henry Wallace. He undertook a cabal to keep Wallace out of office. The nomination of Truman was not so much a pro-Truman proposition as an anti-Wallace affair.

Pauley connived with the president's appointments secretary Maj. Gen. Edwin M. "Pa" Watson to allow only people who were against Henry Wallace to talk to the president prior to the Chicago convention. In Pauley's cabal were notable additions: Postmaster General Frank Walker, who was the former chairman of the national committee; the then-chairman Robert E. Hannegan; the secretary of the committee George E. Allen; Edward J. Flynn, the boss of the Bronx; and the mayor of Chicago Edward J. Kelly.

None of these individuals felt Roosevelt could finish a full fourth term. They believed he had a terminal illness, were not sure what sort of illness was afflicting him, but saw his energy flagging, that he was perpetually tired and his hands shook. In their minds these signs pointed to cancer. In fact, the president was suffering from congestive heart failure and very high blood pressure. His systolic pressure in December 1944 went to 260, and his diastolic was high, too.

They did not know this, but knew he was ill and drew the right conclusion—that he would not survive a fourth term. They knew he would be elected and felt it was absolutely necessary that the vice presidency go to a reliable political man who, because of the elimination of others in what was a rather small field, turned out to be Senator Truman of Missouri.

They were Irish-Catholic politicians and were good men, honest in the way of political bosses. A few votes might be bought now and then, but they had the future of the Republic as their concern, and acted out of that.

I don't believe they thought they could control Truman; they believed he felt the same way they did, and in fact such was true. This was a political point of view. There were compromises that were necessary, nonetheless it was necessary to work for the good of the country. They did not think a politician was necessarily a crooked man, that the word was reprehensible. They were honorable and again, to the question as to whether they thought they could control Truman, it wasn't necessary to control Truman. They all thought the same way.

In early 1944 Roosevelt did not know what was ailing him. He was getting his medical advice from Vice Adm. Ross T. McIntire, who I think was a very poor physician. He was long out of practice, a medical bureaucrat by 1944, managing a huge naval medical corps that numbered 175,000 people. The wonder was he had any time to see the president.

He did not know what was ailing Roosevelt and told the president he was suffering from bronchitis, which was true enough. The problem was that his lungs were congested because his heart could not empty them. To this diagnosis of bronchitis McIntire occasionally added influenza, and then something he described as post-flu. Roosevelt, I think, believed this until Lt. Cmdr. Howard Bruenn, a skilled cardiologist, saw Roosevelt for the first time on March 28, 1944, and was horrified by the president's condition.

Bruen diagnosed it and treated it with digitalis and recommended rest. And, of course, the president was not willing to undertake the rest. For a while the digitalis strengthened the heart muscle and helped the president, but then the basic problem, the weakness of the president's entire cardiovascular system, took over, and eventually killed him on April 12, 1945.

Truman played his hand marvelously in seeking the vice presidential nomination. David McCullough believes, and many other historians agree, that Truman did not want the vice presidential nomination. Mr. Truman often said that. Alben Barkley, a very intelligent, bright fellow, the long-time senator from Kentucky, FDR's majority leader, Truman's vice president in 1949-53, knew better. On onc occasion, in a public affair after a large dinner, [he] chided Truman on that point.

In actual fact, Truman wanted the nomination. Any politician would have wanted it considering what was at stake: the presidency. But he had to be careful for two reasons: One, if he pushed his candidacy in the way Wallace and particularly Byrnes pushed theirs, Roosevelt, who did not like ambitious people, quite possibly would have moved against him. Two, Truman's wife did not want her husband to become vice president and then, as she, as well as Mr. Truman knew, president of the United States.

The whole business of maneuvering the president into accepting Truman was difficult. Mr. Roosevelt didn't know Truman well. But the biggest difficulty for the anti-Wallace group was that they had to be extremely careful in moving FDR against Wallace; they couldn't do it openly. They couldn't say Mr. Roosevelt was ill and was not likely to survive a fourth term. The president was immensely powerful politically and would have taken scalps for such remarks and could have done it because he controlled the party mechanism. Not a single member of the group, not a single political boss, could have stood against the president.

They had to move by indirection, and it was a very difficult and dangerous thing because if word had gotten back—which, fortunately, it did not—that Pauley, Pa Watson, Frank Walker, Bob Hannegan, George Allen, Ed Flynn and Ed Kelly were trying to push Wallace out and put Truman in because they believed the president was not going to live very long, there would have been the very devil to pay.

I don't believe the approaching, almost eminent trouble with the Soviet Union was the governing reason for maneuvering Wallace out of the vice presidency. The reason was his political ineptitude, and secondarily that on American domestic issues he was what his critics would have described as socialistic. It was domestic reasoning, the political incapacity, also the sense that in the business of post-war reconstruction he would be anti-business. If not that, then at least in favor of New Deal measures that to these somewhat conservative political leaders seemed on the verge of going too far.

The Republican candidate in 1944, Thomas E. Dewey, would have made a good president. The only problem being that he lacked what a later generation called charisma. He was not good at demonstrating that he liked people. I'm not sure that he liked people. This flaw in his personality—administratively he was excellent—might have made his presidency difficult.

Truman possessed personal qualities that were remarkable. He was extraordinarily intelligent. He had honed his political abilities over twenty years of American domestic politics and he could think clearly and quickly. He had the ability to take himself out of any political decision. He could look at a problem, analyze it coldly, remove his own personal desires, and make a decision.

It was so fortunate for the country that President Truman was a man with these qualities, rather than some of the other presidents who have graced and disgraced the presidency during recent decades.

CHAPTER 12

Winston Churchill

John Harris

"From Stettin in the Baltic to Trieste in the Adriatic an Iron
Curtain has descended across the Continent."
—Winston Churchill
March 5, 1946
Fulton, Missouri

I was discharged from the Navy in December 1945 and went back to
Fulton, Missouri, my hometown. I was there when the Churchill
[speech] occurred and it caused great excitement.

Harry Truman's military aide, Harry Vaughn, was an alumnus of
Westminster College. When the president of Westminster, Frank
McClure, conceived the idea of asking Mr. Churchill to come here
and speak at what was called a Green Foundation Lecture—there was
one almost every year—he contacted Harry Vaughn and asked if he
would speak to the president and see if the resident would forward
to Mr. Churchill an invitation to speak on the Westminster campus.

The president of Westminster sent a letter to Mr. Truman, a letter
addressed to Churchill, and President Truman endorsed the letter,
saying, "This is a great little college in my home state. If you will
come, I will introduce you." That was the inducement that brought
Mr. Churchill here.

They came by train to Jefferson City. They picked up the governor in
Jefferson City and arrived in Fulton with a cavalcade led by highway
patrolmen on motorcycles. It was quite a spectacle, the town jam-packed
with people. The speech was delivered in the college gymnasium. They
didn't have an auditorium suitable for that size crowd. The gymnasium

was fitted with bleachers almost to the roof. Churchill was introduced by President Truman. It wasn't a long speech, maybe twenty minutes.

The "Iron Curtain" reference was not in the original text.

He injected it later. There was a man in the audience named Howard Lang, a court reporter. He was transcribing the speech as Churchill delivered it and picked up on the Iron Curtain phrase and delivered it to the newspapers. It was not in the prior release of the speech.

It was a receptive audience, obviously, polite applause when indicated, and it went very smoothly. We had a pretty clear notion of the situation regarding Russia before Mr. Churchill made his speech here. I don't think it came as a great shock to anybody that he pointed out the danger that Russia posed. With that kind of a forum and the publicity he received, a person of his prestige made people sit up and take notice. This indeed was a turning point in our international relations with Great Britain and Russia.

Afterward Truman didn't endorse what Mr. Churchill had said. I think he wanted to think about it a bit because it certainly made you wonder what the future of international relations was going to be.

After the speech I heard people commenting on what a marvelous presentation it was and what a fine orator Mr. Churchill was. That was the feeling everybody had, a great occasion, a wonderful thing to happen in Fulton, Mr. Churchill a great man.

Mr. Churchill was no longer prime minister. He had been voted out of office. The idea that he would be accompanied by, and introduced by, the president of the United States gave him a platform with much visibility in this country and in his own country.

In the early sixties, the president of Westminster College, Larry Davidson, conceived the idea of constructing on the Westminster campus a memorial to Winston Churchill's appearance. The idea gathered momentum and to make a long story short, the outcome was that a Christopher Wren church, which was in downtown London and had been bombed during the war, was going to be razed because the parish had no further use for it. Through arrangements, contributions, and help from many directions, the church was dismantled and re-erected on the Westminster campus.

It's called the Church of St. Mary the Virgin Aldermanberry. It's an elegant little building, refitted totally in that period, has an organ, and in the undercroft is the museum and library. This is the Churchill Memorial.

CHAPTER 13

The Cold War

John L. Gaddis

This noted historian is the author of *The United States and the Origins of the Cold War, Strategies of Containment, The Long Peace,* and *The United States and the End of the Cold War.* He believes that as long as Stalin was running the Soviet Union it would have been difficult to avoid the Cold War, and that Eisenhower was more effective than Truman in fighting communism because he initiated more ideas. Truman appointed excellent people but originated few ideas himself.

Gaddis thinks that Stalin and Khrushchev were poor leaders and contributed mightily to our cause because of their incompetence. Everything Stalin did to provoke us we countered, and this produced results detrimental to the Soviet Union.

I think it would have been very difficult to avoid the Cold War as long as Stalin was running the Soviet Union. It's one of those situations where history comes down to a matter of individual personalities. Stalin had a concept of security, both national and personal, that involved maintaining a Cold War against everybody, whether inside Russia or outside, and as long as you had him in charge it would have been very difficult to avoid. If there had been somebody else in charge it might have been quite a different proposition.

He had always thought in terms of a Cold War because his whole career had been based on distrust and suspicion. Much of the key to understanding Stalin is to project his behavior inside the Soviet Union onto the world scene when he becomes concerned about issues of foreign policy. A good deal of this was ingrained, programmed into him. Look how far he was thinking ahead. For example, the decision to plant spies in Britain and the U.S. in the thirties. That's somebody who is not looking forward to an amicable and trustful relationship.

Nineteen forty-five is important if you are an international relations theorist because it's one of the two or three times in the last five hundred years that the international system has fundamentally and dramatically changed. If you're a student of military history it's important because the war ended. If you're a student of nuclear history it's important because nuclear weapons are invented in that period. And if you're a student of cold war history it's important because that's when the Cold War really starts. Take your pick.

We know Hitler was prepared to risk war and indeed may well have relished the prospect of it. With Stalin you have a very different pattern. Ultimately he believed in the inevitability of some kind of war between the communist world and the capitalist world. He was quite a traditional Marxist/Leninist in that regard.

But he saw that as a fairly distant prospect because he was also very well aware of the weakness of the Soviet Union after World War II. No matter what you look at, whether it's Berlin, Korea, or others, we see a tendency to take risks where he thought he could get away with it, but when challenged, to pull back. He's kind of like a schoolyard bully who goads other people, but then backs down when challenged. Some of the documentation that has come out of the Soviet Union, particularly on Korea, is sustaining that.

I don't think there would have been a Soviet invasion of Europe because I don't think that was realistically in the cards. But that's not the reason the Truman Doctrine and the Marshall Plan were put in in the first place. They were put in because of the danger of psychological collapse, psychological demoralization in Europe, and that was a very real prospect at the time.

I think it's entirely possible that you could have had a situation in which the Europeans would have become so demoralized that they might have become desperate and voted in their own communist parties, which were large in countries like France and Italy. That in turn would have provided a considerable avenue of influence for Stalin because these were still loyal parties at that time. Nobody can prove this, and there is a lot of disagreement among historians, but there are those who say the European economy was improving and would have improved in the absence of the Marshall Plan.

I am skeptical because I'm reluctant to look at things solely in economic terms. I think psychology is important.

*What if the communist bloc had accepted the Marshall Plan?
Czechoslovakia wanted it but Stalin killed it.*

Well, it's interesting. It was more seriously considered in Moscow
than many of us had thought. We now know from Soviet documentation that Stalin's first inclination was to accept it because he was
looking at it in Marxist [terms] and believed it was a sign of the coming economic crash in the United States. That the U.S. was desperate
to find and revive overseas markets. He had his own peculiar way of
looking at this.

The first instinct, we now know, was actually to accept it, but then
very quickly he does a double take and decides that no, the real
[American] objective is to try to pull the East Europeans away from
Soviet influence, which was accurate enough.

To pull the East Europeans out of the Soviet Bloc and bring them
within an American sphere of influence was one of the secondary
motives, apart from the basic Western European recovery from the
Marshall Plan. If they had accepted it, almost certainly it would have
accelerated Titoist tendencies already evident in Eastern Europe. But
if the Soviet Union had accepted it, there's a real possibility it would
never had been passed by the Congress. That's where Stalin probably
really blew it because if he had accepted on behalf of the Soviet
Union, it would have posed a real dilemma for the Truman
Administration, which would have had a terrible time getting it
through the Congress.

Truman's main [strength] [was] putting good people in positions
of responsibility in foreign policy and national security policy. I
would make the argument that Truman had less to do with the shaping of foreign policy in his administration than Eisenhower did later
on. Eisenhower was a good deal more influential than Dulles.

Under Truman, it was his subordinates, people like Marshall,
Kennan, and Acheson, where the ideas came from. Truman had the
good sense to bring intelligent people in, give them authority, and listen to them. I don't see him as someone who initiated the fundamental ideas, but he certainly had the ultimate responsibility that
made it possible.

Eisenhower was a much more sophisticated thinker than Truman
regarding foreign policy and military policy and a lot more experienced in that regard. Some of the fundamental elements of strategy

in the Eisenhower period—the emphasis on nuclear deterrents, the emphasis on balancing the budget and on limiting expenditures for national security—are very much Eisenhower's personal ideas. He liked to give the impression of being a lightweight and to convey the impression that the fundamental ideas were flowing from Dulles or other people. But it's clear from the archives that Eisenhower was much more on top of things and the source of ideas within his administration than Truman was.

We were lucky in having reasonably good leadership in that period. I don't think we had very many people who got to the top who did dumb things. We had a real advantage in comparison to the leadership of the Soviet Union. One of the things that is going to stand out more and more clearly as we look back at the Soviet experience [is] just how bad their leadership was all the way through, not just Stalin, but Khrushchev and Brezhnev as well.

Part of the reason is that an authoritarian system doesn't provide an adequate means of training or replacing leaders. It doesn't provide good grounds for preparation for statecraft, and it certainly doesn't give you a way of getting rid of incompetents in the way that exists in a democratic system. Even with all the differences between Truman and Eisenhower and between Dulles and Acheson and so on, we were fortunate that we had people who had a fair amount of good sense.

If I were to give credit to any individual for the implementation of American Cold War policies—the Truman Doctrine, the Marshall Plan, NATO, re-armament of Germany, NSC-68 [Policy Paper No. 68 of the National Security Council; it was an integral part of the Truman Doctrine in fighting the Cold War]—I would give Stalin the credit. Almost [all], in one way or another, resulted from some provocation on Stalin's part. One has to wonder, looking back on it all—particularly the Czech coup, the Berlin Blockade, and the authorization to Kim Il-Sung to invade South Korea—what kind of an intelligence system this guy had. Presumably he had a pretty good intelligence system, because he had very highly placed spies.

Obviously he wasn't using his intelligence well because every one of those things backfired on him, every one produced results that were not what he intended. They either produced the Marshall Plan, or NATO, or American re-armament, or the Tito defection, or whatever. None of these things could have been what Stalin wanted. Here is somebody who really blew it.

The same is true of Khrushchev, though not quite to the same extent. With Khrushchev, you've got somebody who is in many ways even more dangerous than Stalin because he was more of a risk-taker. He put missiles into Cuba, which I doubt Stalin would have done. But at the same time, unlike Stalin, Khrushchev really wanted to find a way to end the Cold War. He really did believe in peaceful co-existence, but certainly had a counter-productive way of going about it.

What is going to be remembered about Khrushchev is not so much that he tried to dismantle the Stalinist system, but that he actually failed to the extent he did. It's not an impressive record of leadership on the Soviet side.

The Marshall Plan was the single most effective thing we did in terms of accomplishing the maximum possible results for a relatively minimal investment. This worked best.

I believe our government thought if containment was implemented, if the West re-armed, the Russians would not start a war, and eventually the internal contradictions of their system would bring it down. I don't think anybody expected it would take forty-five years for that to happen. We were expecting it would happen sooner than that, but it never became a sufficiently realistic prospect that people thought in detail how it was going to happen.

By the time Eisenhower comes in, people are settling down to the idea it's going to be a permanent condition, [with] Eisenhower looking toward ways to make it safer. But they lose sight that ultimately communism would collapse.

I think you have to ask about the costs. Could we have done it more effectively? Could we have done it more cheaply? There were a lot of things we didn't need to do, like Vietnam. Gross distortions, distractions away from the main event.

CHAPTER 14

Jackie Robinson's Ordeal

Carl Erskine

The first black to play in the major leagues was Fleet Walker. He played in forty-two games for Toledo in the American Association in 1884. His brother, Welday, joined him later that same year and played in five games. Back then, Toledo was in the big leagues. Bing Miller, Armando Marsans, George Treadway, Bill Higgins, and Tommy de la Cruz are among a limited number of players who also played in the majors and were supposed to have been partly black. But until 1947, no one discernibly black had played in the major leagues since the Walkers.

Jackie Robinson joined the Brooklyn Dodgers as a twenty-eight-year-old rookie in 1947. He was talented, black, and a target for every racial epithet known in the Western world. Much of America was not integrated in 1947; therefore, a black man playing first base for Brooklyn did not bring out the best in some segments of the population, especially opposing teams, fans, and for that matter a few of Robinson's teammates.

Carl Erskine came up to the Brooklyn Dodgers in 1948 and proceeded to become one of baseball's top pitchers. He played with Jackie from 1948 through the 1956 season, when Robinson retired. They were friends.

Jackie introduced himself to me in 1948 while I was on the Ft. Worth roster; Ft. Worth was a Double-A farm team of the Dodgers. The big club came through there in the spring and I pitched three innings. When the game was over Robinson, came over to our dugout and looked me up. I didn't know Jackie. I didn't know anybody on the big club, and he said, "Young man, you're not going to be down here very long. You're going to be with us before long."

Well, by July of that year the Dodgers did call me up. I'd won fifteen at Ft. Worth and they needed pitching. Robinson came over to me as I walked in the clubhouse in Pittsburgh, stuck out his hand, the first one to do that, and said, "I was right. I told you you'd be here." That set the stage for a strong friendship, as well as [our] being teammates for the next nine years.

We were good friends, and were together off the field some. Pee Wee Reese, Ralph Branca, Clem Labine, and others were genuinely respectful of Jackie and considered him to be a class person, and I'm sure they consider him to this day a close friend. Jackie and I had a special relationship because he thought I went out of my way [for him] on a couple of occasions, which truthfully I did not, and told him so.

There was an area in Ebbets Field that was fenced off in which our families, or close friends who were authorized, could wait protected from the push of the crowd. We'd open that gate and go through to get to our cars or whatever. I came out one day and Rachel, Jackie's wife, and their young son, Jackie Junior, who was probably eight years old, were standing outside, and I went over to Rachel and spoke to her and talked to young Jackie for a few minutes and then went on my way.

The next day Jackie came to my locker and said, "Carl, I want to thank you for that yesterday."

I said, "What's that?"

"Well," he said, "in front of all those fans you went over and spent some time with Rachel and Jackie."

I said, "Jackie, you can't thank me for that. I didn't do anything unusual. Just seemed natural to me, and your family's a beautiful family."

But he thought that was an extension of myself that was intended to help him. I hope it did help him. But I said, "You compliment me on a good pitch or a well-pitched inning or something, but I can't take credit for that."

You know, Mr. Rickey [Branch Rickey, the general manager of the Dodgers who signed Robinson] was a very smart and sensitive man in reading people. Mr. Rickey always called this try with Jackie an experiment and wasn't sure it would work. As soon as Jackie got to the big leagues and they saw what kind of ability he had, and he was winning ball games for us with his bat, his glove, and, of course, his running ability, they quickly respected Jackie and understood he was big-league caliber. That in itself took the color out of the picture, more or less.

Now there was always kidding. If you had a big nose or a funny walk, or a long neck, you got the business. Not only from the fans, but from your teammates. But in a sense that is total acceptance when you can do that, and Jackie fit in. In the first two or three years we were awestruck to be in the big leagues. We were all young and battling for our jobs. I don't think we had as much concern for Jackie sometimes as we did, *Am I going to make it this year?*

The crowds in some ballparks were segregated in those days; hard to imagine, but in the South we were always segregated. The black fans were totally of course for Jackie, and the white fans, sometimes you wondered if the score meant anything. If Jackie made a good play, the blacks would cheer, and if he happened to make an error or get thrown out at a base, whites would erupt. It was that kind of atmosphere. But on our bench, in our clubhouse, I didn't see any, or hear any remarks that were seriously opposed to Jackie's being there.

We came through the South and on more than one occasion coming north, and maybe it happened during the season in the early years, Jackie would get threatening letters sent to the ballpark: "If you take the field, you're going to be shot."

I remember them reading one of those in the clubhouse in Atlanta one day. We always stopped and played two or three days in Atlanta on the way north. In the early years, they wouldn't let the blacks even buy a ticket. They sat on the levee behind the rightfield fence and watched the game. They could not get into the ballpark. The Klan picketed the hotel on one occasion, and they, of course, wrote threatening letters.

Burt Shotton [Dodger manager] in about '49 read a threatening letter to Jackie: "If you take the field you're going to be shot." It got quiet in the clubhouse and everybody was pretty sober. Finally, Gene Hermanski says, "Hey, Skip, I've got an idea. If all of us wore number 42 they wouldn't know who to shoot at."

Well, that broke up everybody, and we go out on the field, and I remember warming up along the sidelines waiting for battling practice to start, and Pee Wee Reese is saying to Jackie, "Hey, Jackie, do you mind getting over a little farther? I mean, after all, it might bounce offa you and hit me."

That was the mood of the players. Yeah, this is serious, but it spoke to Jackie's total acceptance.

I always felt that Reese was the perfect guy to play shortstop with Jackie because he had great respect in the league. But nobody talks about the guy on the other side of Jackie—Gil Hodges—who had extreme respect in the league. I think Gil Hodges, with his temperament and respect among fans and players, created an atmosphere that defused some problems for Jackie.

Gil was a great peacemaker. If there was a confrontation at second base involving Jackie, Gil was right there and broke it up quickly. I don't think you have any recorded incidents in which Jackie was in a fistfight, but there were plenty of times it was provoked. I know Mr. Rickey had an agreement with Jackie that for two years he would turn the other check and not make any motion of retaliation, even an expression. He was to get up, dust himself off, and not make any indication he wanted to retaliate.

There was an air of caution around Jackie. There were a few people totally against the idea, a few people totally in favor of the idea. But there was a whole raft of people in the middle who were neutral and wanted to see if this was going to work or not before they took a position.

Was Robinson the best man available to break the "barrier"?

Well, number one, he did it. There could have been others who might have done it differently. [Roy] Campanella certainly was a superstar, and he had a totally different attitude about it than Jackie did. I think if Campy had done it, it would have come out differently.

There were some fifty screened black athletes that the scouting system of the Dodgers had identified as potential. My understanding is Mr. Rickey led his scouting staff to believe he was considering the Brooklyn Brown Dodgers, a team to play in the Negro League, and when Robinson came to be interviewed he thought that's what the interview was about, only to find he'd been selected.

I didn't have any feeling that Willie Mays or somebody else could have done it better. Mr. Rickey, if he had a strength beyond [being] a good general manager, [having] a good baseball mind, if he had an intuitive strength, it was in reading the character of people he kept and the people he traded.

I went through an exhibit that Coca-Cola helped put together with the New York Museum of History—a traveling museum of Jackie Robinson's life. They assigned a *Sports Illustrated* writer to walk around with me and get my reaction since I'd played with Jackie.

It was a beautiful experience. They had tapes playing, had quotes printed on some of these exhibits, had pictures of Jackie and so on. I came to one and it was a quote by Jackie's mother. I got to thinking about that. He was born, I believe, in Alabama [actually, in Georgia] and then moved to the West Coast. The indication was that his mother was a very strong Christian person. She talked to them constantly about the dignity of their life.

Jackie was a college graduate. Most of us had not gone to college in those days. It was rare to find a college grad in pro baseball. But Robinson was an intelligent person.

When I saw this illustration of his mother, I knew Mr. Rickey's convictions as a Christian person. He took a lot of heat for that. People said he was a hypocrite. He wouldn't come to the ballpark on Sunday, but he didn't mind selling out a doubleheader. But I think Rickey tried to apply what his mother had been strong in as he grew up a farm boy in Ohio.

Suddenly, a light went on: That's why he picked Robinson. The training Robinson had had from his mother, instilling in him the dignity of a human being, and the education Jackie received overrode in Rickey's mind his militancy, his combativeness, and I believe Mr. Rickey [thought]: *Here's a man who'll understand what we're trying to do. He'll have enough self-control and is intelligent enough to read what's happening and be able to make it work.*

The ball club didn't win by virtue of any one person, as no club can. But Jackie brought a dimension to that talented team that maybe had only been there in part in previous years. Jackie brought an intensity to win. The Dodgers had won on occasion but they never had a sustained decade until the "Robinson Decade."

The difference in us being a contender or being a winner could well have been Jackie's intensity. Even when he was past his peak and couldn't play every day, he would save himself for the big games, the big series. He would go on the field against Milwaukee when they were contenders; Jackie would tell these guys, "Hey, I'm in there today. I want you to know I'm playing. I rested two days for this series." He would intimidate the opposition and that would lift us.

Did he look on himself as a crusader, or a ballplayer, or both?

I think both. Jackie was a natural athlete. He loved to play. He loved to win. He had all those qualities. But when he was selected to be THE first black, I think Jackie put a mantle on himself. Maybe he didn't put it on himself. It was there. What he did was so critical to what would happen after him that he couldn't afford to fail. And yet, Jackie was human. He didn't hit .600, he didn't do something nobody else had ever done. But he did qualify to be a major leaguer and a Hall of Famer.

But Jackie's other side of life was never satisfied, and I'm not sure it was ever even closely satisfied. He used to take strong exception when people would say to him, "Boy, Jackie, you've made it. You've really done it. You've broken the line. You're here. You're established. You're going to be in the Hall of Fame."

He'd take strong exception to that and say, "Wait a minute. That's nothing to what needs to be done. I haven't even scratched the surface." I think he went to his grave with that on his lips: *Don't tell me how I made it.*

History is big. Jackie's part was big, but it was just a small piece of the whole picture. I told Jackie, "Jackie, you know you've helped your race tremendously. But you helped my race a lot more." I believe that. He opened a new understanding, a new sensitivity that people had, but was buried in the culture of the time—that's the way it had always been done—and the extremists in the racial picture had the upper hand. Jackie, through sports, did what is the ideal way to earn a place in the work force, in the sports picture or whatever.

I take exception to some degree to laws that force acceptance, where[as] Jackie, when given the chance, proved he belonged. Nobody took exception to that. You never heard anybody say, "Hey, he got to the big leagues on the color of his skin. They had to have a black and he was it." No, he earned it and everybody respected that. To me, that is the right way to do it, and I'm real proud baseball was the stage on which it was presented and proven to be the right way.

PART II

This Is the Beginning of the End

(Tallyrand)

CHAPTER 15

Joe McCarthy

William F. Buckley, Jr.

The roots of today's conservative movement can be traced to William F. Buckley, Jr. His efforts at *The National Review*, books such as *God and Man at Yale*, as a columnist, television commentator, and debater gave an intellectual implication to a cause hurt by Joe McCarthy's irresponsible actions. For a long while Buckley carried the conservative movement.

Some consider the period in America from 1946 to the mid-fifties an impassioned time because of the communist menace. Russia broke the Yalta Agreements and began taking over Eastern Europe. There was the Berlin Airlift, Alger Hiss, China's going communist, Judith Copeland, and Russia's exploding of their first atomic bomb—all of this occurring before 1950. In light of these developments it really was not an overreaction.

I agree wholeheartedly. Society just finished engaging in a world war. A society that had to rouse itself from its natural posture of isolationism to engage in that war in the first instance, to confront weapons apocalyptic in their implications, and to learn that some of the vital information respecting the development of those weapons was being given by Americans to Soviet agents contribute to the state of concern you just finished describing.

Joe McCarthy walked into this. He made a speech in February 1950 in Wheeling, West Virginia claiming there were 205 communists in the State Department. Why McCarthy? Why didn't someone else come to the fore?

He simply turned out to be somebody useful to congressional investigators who felt we were doing a lousy job in loyalty/security, and then it bounced off McCarthy and he became sort of the central figure in that fight. I don't think there's any reason to suppose that he was especially equipped or had a special background that would have normally led him to be the principal figurehead in that instance.

He simply wasn't very conspicuous. He was considered a liberal Republican and he had no particular constituency. He had been, interestingly enough, exercised on the question of the Russian massacre of Polish officers [in the Katyn Forest].

It wasn't so much that the Republicans elevated him to a position of leadership on that particular issue. It's that he showed he had certain skills which were highly communicable, and he gathered his own constituency, and therefore the Republican Party substantially flocked to him.

He had no boundaries, which alarmed and angered many people.

I think people were alarmed for several reasons. For one thing, he picked on a lot of people who were icons in America. General Marshall was one example. For another, he challenged the whole position of the Establishment in their handling of loyalty/security questions. So for that reason, they were sort of corporately affronted. You may remember at that point, Harry Truman was refusing to believe Alger Hiss was guilty. There was a general sentiment abroad that we were dealing with invincible ignorance.

Many people thought Hiss guilty.

Well, it was a feeling in the "outback." It was certainly not the feeling in the centers of the intellectual capitals. I would say at the time Hiss was convicted, probably 50 percent of the faculty at the school I was at [Yale] thought him innocent. They were liberal intellectuals. They were people who were passionately passive defenders of Rooseveltian diplomacy and didn't want to think that somebody who was not exactly critical to the formation of that diplomacy, nevertheless very well situated there, should have in fact been an agent of the enemy.

What was McCarthy's undoing?

I think [McCarthy] was driven toward generalizations, which he could not back up. Then he made the critical mistake of accusing the Army. The Army has always been a central and sacred institution, and in doing so he alienated a lot of his own supporters. This tended also to coincide with a period of personal decomposition. He became an alcoholic, lost his judgment, and under the circumstances suddenly became unconvincing.

He was finally thought of by a number of Republicans as having gone too far. And, of course, he made that rather disastrous speech in which he accused them of being handmaidens of American communism and that served to alienate quite a few of them.

During that period, several of them concluded McCarthy had gone too far and that association with him at the extremes he had gone to would be personally dangerous to them politically, and therefore there were defections.

The one that hurt him the most was the senator from Delaware [John J. Williams], the man of great probity who had been very pro-McCarthy up until that moment.

Eisenhower loathed McCarthy and had a public dispute with him. Eisenhower simply suspended all diplomatic communications with him, didn't invite him to the White House, even for regular receptions, so it was pretty much open warfare between the two. Not a very good idea for a senator who wants to survive.

Was McCarthy at all effective?

I think initially, yes. And I think ultimately, no. The cause of anti-anti-communism prospered as the result of the excesses of McCarthy, which bred excesses greater than his own, which is the thesis of my book *McCarthy and His Enemies*.

I think he did good. What I'm prepared to say is whether the good that he did was followed by activity that damaged America, which activity drew life from McCarthy's own excesses. In other words, he encouraged an anti-McCarthyism of a kind that went so far as to nearly destroy our loyalty/security system in the years immediately after he made all that noise.

If I had to say at this point would American anti-communism been better off or worse off had he never lived, I would be driven to the conclusion that it would have been better off if he had not lived. However, I hold him only partly responsible for this.

I hold the intellectual community substantially responsible because their overreaction was pretty indefensible. When you have people like Robert Maynard Hutchins saying that it took an act of physical bravery to contribute money to Harvard University because of McCarthy, then you know that there's an imbalance there, for which McCarthy could hardly be held responsible.

CHAPTER 16

The McCarthy Era

Richard Fried

By 1950 the country was in the grip of a "Red Scare." Communism was an inexorable force affecting the national equilibrium. Many were looking for someone to right the situation, and since Joe McCarthy needed an issue to help get re-elected to the Senate, he ran with the communist threat for all it was worth. It was worth a lot for four years, but then he overstepped himself. Richard Fried wrote *Nightmare in Red: The McCarthy Era in Perspective*. He is a professor of recent American history at the University of Illinois at Chicago.

There was a great deal of anxiety that had developed by the early 1950s in the wake of the Cold War. One could say the "High Cold War," if you want to call it that, began with the Korean War in June 1950. But even before, international problems had produced domestic tensions in the United States.

Before McCarthy came on the scene, you had most of the makings of a communist scare. You had two world wars with two red scares following them. One could say we haven't had any other red scares. I would argue we had at least a mini-red scare in the late 1930s, but that's on the doorstep of World War II and is related to it. The only other case of a scare might be in the early Reagan years, and that just didn't take off. That soufflé did not rise.

By 1950 you've got a pretty clear perception on the part of the American public that we face a hostile enemy in the Soviet Union. It's an expansive enemy, it's dangerous. The term "Iron Curtain" had entered the language. We hadn't had a shooting war as yet, but there had been tension over the Berlin Crisis in 1948; certainly the Greek civil war was hot.

In 1947 the federal government imposed a loyalty program. It wasn't the first. There had been a loyalty program in 1942 during World War II. Truman's Executive Order 9835 strengthened it, formalized it, institutionalized it, and made it a part of everyone's life who served in the federal government.

The loyalty issue was entering politics. The Hiss-Chambers confrontation took place in the context of the 1948 election, and it was perhaps a stroke of luck for the Democrats that the timing didn't affect the outcome. But when after two trials Hiss was found guilty of perjury in January 1950, that seemed to validate a lot of unfocused, but pretty intense feeling on the part of conservatives that there had been something rotten with the New Deal. And now Hiss seemed to be proof of that.

In 1949 you not only had the Hiss trial, but the fall of China to the forces of Mao Tse-tung. To some people, this was not a normal event. There had to be some dirty work at the crossroads, so there was a search for scapegoats in the State Department. You had an attempt to purge the "China Hands" from the State Department; they had presumably "un-done" Chiang Kai-shek.

The other big event of 1949 was the Soviets had detonated an atomic bomb, so the atomic monopoly we enjoyed for four years was gone. That was quite unsettling. You had a couple of other spy episodes in 1949, so the front-page news was almost locked in. You could expect weekly something regarding the Soviet threat, something about Soviet agents, spies, and so forth. That was the context into which McCarthy jumped with both feet in February 1950.

Perhaps there would have been no McCarthy if it hadn't been for the political dynamic that prevailed when he came along. The communist issue was a handy club for the Republican Party to use against the Democrats who, in some ungodly fashion, from the Republican point of view, had managed to win five presidential elections in a row and control Congress except for one two-year period after 1946. So there's a sense of "what can we do to get these guys out of here."

Perhaps that sounds cynical, but these were cynical days. But for many years people have seen McCarthy as a phenomenon that has to be explained by the political ambitions of people in his party, and also the ambitions of a particular wing of the Republican Party, the conservatives.

The Republican Party was divided. Some would say the division was almost geographic. You've got the Midwest and the Mountain States versus the Coasts. It's also a foreign policy outlook, and it's not just coincidental that there was more isolationism—residual isolationism—among Republicans in the hinterland than there was on the East and West coasts. You've got governors in 1950 like Tom Dewey of New York and Earl Warren of California who were as interventionist as the Truman Administration. You had Republican interventionists in 1940; Roosevelt took some of them into his cabinet.

McCarthy and his issue represent a kind of battering ram by people who've been out of power in their party. If you look at the nominations—Willkie, Dewey, Eisenhower—all of them are internationalists. All of them, according to the right wing, are apologists for the New Deal. The title of Phyllis Schlafly's 1964 book, *A Choice Not an Echo,* deals with the fact that the Republicans will win if they come up with a full-blown conservative, not just a pale echo of the New Deal.

So McCarthy, not necessarily sharing all the views of that group of the party, becomes their battering ram. McCarthy actually was kind of an interventionist on foreign policy issues.

Edward R. Murrow confronted him via network television on March 9, 1954. Who had taken a national stance against McCarthy prior to that?

That's a famous event, and a lot of people assume that McCarthy's decline began as a result of Murrow's exposing him by editing film clips that indicated McCarthy at his worst.

Not on TV, which was not quite the medium that we know today, but on radio there was Elmer Davis. You can go through Davis' scripts . . . from 1950 on he realized McCarthy was bad medicine for the country. Martin Agronsky had also taken on McCarthy. Drew Pearson had a radio program, he had a column. Pearson had been friendly with Joe before 1950, but they had a cat-and-dog fight.

Murrow was not the first. He had an on-screen gravity, people respected and trusted him, it had impact. As much as anything it was a signal that the tide was running out on McCarthy because the Murrow program happened in March, the same time roughly that

Adlai Stevenson gave a major speech attacking McCarthy and accusing the Republicans of being half Eisenhower and half McCarthy.

The Army-McCarthy Hearings began April 22, 1954, and with it the eventual confrontation between McCarthy and Joseph Welch. They had made an agreement that Fred Fisher, a member of Welch's law firm, would not be mentioned as once having belonged to the Lawyers Guild, a leftist organization. The quid pro quo was Welch would not mention Roy Cohn's lack of military service. McCarthy broke the bargain. He mentioned Fisher—and Welch was ready.

Nobody's been able to prove it was the Army Hearings that did McCarthy in. It makes a dramatic story, a very dramatic confrontation between Welch and McCarthy. You can see Roy Cohn trying to mouth the word "no" when McCarthy takes up the Fisher business. There are those who argue that Welch was hoping this would happen.

That little homily he gave was too smooth, one might almost say rehearsed. Everyone assumed that it was spontaneous, but there are those who argue that Welch was ready and waiting.

Something subtle happened; McCarthy does go down in the polls. He stood at 50 percent favorable ratings in January 1954, and at the end of the Army-McCarthy Hearings in June, he is at 34 percent. But 34 percent is still a lot of people. There are not a whole lot of senators that would want to go against 34 percent of the public and anger them, because those people vote. The shift is pretty subtle. It becomes clear to some Republicans that McCarthy is no longer a useful partisan weapon because it doesn't seem to matter to him who's in the White House. He always used to talk about twenty years of treason under the Democrats, and he makes a crack about twenty-one years—the twenty-first year being Eisenhower.

One of the subfacts of the McCarthy years . . . there's a little publication called *"Influences On the 1954 Mid-Term Elections"* that was a statistical analysis done by Louis Bean, a statistician and a Democrat. A lot of McCarthy's critics ponied up money to get this published. McCarthy's greatest source of strength was the sense on the part of his colleagues that if you crossed him, you were dead.

Millard Tydings of Maryland, the conservative Democrat, had crossed him in 1950, and McCarthy had intervened in an election everyone thought Tydings should have won. He'd been in the Senate for twenty-four years and an upstart Republican beat him in 1950. William Benton, the liberal Democrat from Connecticut, attacked McCarthy in 1951—tried to have the Senate discipline him—and McCarthy campaigned against Benton in Connecticut, and Benton lost.

McCarthy consciously used the fear of his colleagues in this fashion. So what needed to be proven was that it wasn't that simple. Bean took a look at a number of elections. McCarthy goes into a state in 1952 and if the Democrat lost, McCarthy got credit for the result. But Bean pointed out that the people McCarthy campaigned against ran ahead of the national Democratic ticket. He was not trying to prove that to have McCarthy as an opponent was worth votes, but it almost looked that way.

There's no telling what the influence of that was. I'm not saying it was huge, but you see copies of this pamphlet in a couple of files at the Eisenhower White House. You see it in senators' files. One just wonders. People needed some sort of evidence like that to prove to them that they didn't have to be absolutely gutless in the McCarthy contest.

What was the turning point that led to the undoing of McCarthy?

You'd have to talk about multiple turning points. Little pinpricks that developed opposition to McCarthy in areas where it had previously existed and/or showed that you could, with skillful tactics, face down McCarthy.

In the summer of 1953, McCarthy overstepped himself. He appointed to a staff position on his subcommittee a man named J. B. Matthews. Matthews had been an ordained Methodist minister who'd been far to the left in the 1930s, and then he swung far to the right in the late thirties and became a member of the staff of the Dies' Committee, and then a resident anti-communist for the Hearst papers.

Matthews had a reputation on the right as being a very knowing anti-communist. He had just written an article that said the Protestant clergy in America was riddled with communists and this stuck in some craws. It bothered John McClellan who was a Democratic member of McCarthy's subcommittee, but a very conservative Democrat from Arkansas, a rather Protestant state.

Some of these senators started hearing from clergy, and you got a fairly orchestrated effort to repudiate this appointment. Even the White House got involved. A statement was issued from Ike saying this kind of blanket accusation was not in the American grain. There was a funny backstage race to make sure that this attack on McCarthy by Ike—an oblique attack, but it was clear who it was directed at—got to the press before McCarthy was able to fire Matthews, which was his intention.

At one point Richard Nixon is entertaining McCarthy in his office and asking questions. Nixon is playing a sort of double role, the administration's contact with McCarthy. The point is to slow McCarthy down so he can't announce that Matthews has resigned until the Eisenhower statement gets to the press. That's happening in July 1953.

It's something of a turning point that G. David Schine's draft number comes up in the fall of '53. Cohn, McCarthy, and Frank Carr of McCarthy's subcommittee all try to get the army to do something. Try to keep him from being drafted or try to get him something in the CIA, or as McCarthy once said, "Can't you post him to the Waldorf, where Dave can take care of his girls?" There's this constant infighting between McCarthy and the army on the Schine issue.

There was the issue of what McCarthy alleges is communist infiltration of the Army, particularly the Signal Corps labs at Fort Monmouth, New Jersey. The issues on both sides of that confrontation eventually bring on the Army-McCarthy Hearings in April 1954. It may be a turning point that on January 21, 1954, there's a meeting of important people from Eisenhower's White House staff, the Justice Department, and the army, putting their heads together regarding McCarthy.

The army's counsel, John G. Adams, is the one that's been bearing the brunt of all this pressure about Schine's assignment and whether the names of people who had cleared certain loyalty cases for the army are going to be released to McCarthy or not. This is the point at which the Peress case emerged.

Irving Peress was a dentist who, as doctors and dentists were at that time, was drafted. He took the Fifth on whether he belonged to subversive organizations. When this came out, he'd been promoted to captain, which was in keeping with the law and with his training. So

McCarthy makes a big issue of who promoted Peress. The Army isn't going to finger anyone who is responsible for clearing him. That's the main issue from the McCarthy point of view, and from the army point of view, it's the status of G. David Schine.

So at the January 21st meeting it is agreed Adams should make a written record of all the times he's been hassled by McCarthy and Cohn. It's when that record is leaked in March, and then McCarthy counter-leaks his side of the story, that the hearings become inevitable.

There's one more turning point, and that is a person, as much as an event. It's Ralph Flanders, a very dogged Republican from Vermont. He gave three speeches in the spring of 1954 critical of McCarthy. Finally, he decides his Republican colleagues must take a position on McCarthy, but they do not want that to happen because they think it plays into the hands of the Democrats. They would just as soon sweep all this under the rug, but Flanders in June proposes that McCarthy be removed from his committee posts.

That's unprecedented, and he changes it to a resolution that McCarthy be censured. The foot- draggers say, "Well, you can't just censure somebody. You have to have grounds for that." Flanders comes up with grounds and starts getting help from fellow senators. Wayne Morse proposed a bill of particulars, and so did J. W. Fulbright, the Democrat from Arkansas.

The Senate leadership decides they cannot duck this anymore, although they try again. They appoint a select committee under Arthur Watkins of Utah. The committee starts holding hearings and deliberations in August 1954. People still hope this will go away, but the Watkins Committee comes out with a report, and it's debated and voted on by the Senate after the election of 1954. Nobody wants it to be an issue during the campaign.

McCarthy was censured in December '54. Quickly faded from the scene, and died in May 1957 of alcoholism.

Did he make any contribution at all?

No. He never found a communist. He did unearth a bookie ring in the Government Printing Office. So maybe that's his monument. The McCarthy argument is, "We got Hiss." But "we" was somebody else.

You could further argue, although I don't accept the premise, that McCarthy alerted the American public to this menace. That's what McCarthy's partisans would say. Well, anyone who was alerted by McCarthy had been asleep for the first five years of the Cold War.

CHAPTER 17

The End of School Segregation

David Halberstam

The foundation for the Civil Rights Movement of the 1960s was laid in 1954 with *Brown v. Board of Education*. Pulitzer Prize-winning journalist David Halberstam believes it was the dominant event of the 1950s.

The events which occurred in the sixties were boiling underneath the surface during the fifties. *Brown v. Board of Education* was like throwing a major switch. From this point the social volatility began, but most of it doesn't surface until the early sixties. You get little glimmers of it at Montgomery, and a little bit of a glimmer at Little Rock, but demonstrating in the streets with television covering it doesn't occur until the sixties.

I knew this was taking place because as a young man I left college in 1955 and immediately went down to Mississippi and Tennessee; it had begun by 1954. It was slower, it hadn't exploded, but the forces that would bring change were beginning to come together and be galvanized.

You have the coming of an audacious new group of very confident, articulate, and well-educated black leaders, symbolically led by Martin Luther King. I was there in those days, and there were many other black leaders every bit as gifted as Martin. There was C. T. Vivian, Jim Lawson, Kelly Miller Smith, Wyatt T. Walker. It was a real coming of age for a great group of leaders.

In the past, one of the things that weakened black protest was they went out and nobody made a record of what they were doing. But now, post-*Brown v. Board of Education,* if they went in the streets, white reporters would cover them, and that of course made them more audacious than ever. The nation was wired around '56-'57. Suddenly there was this increasingly confident black leadership and this new instrument called television, each needing the other.

The network news producers needed a good, dramatic, moral story to put on every night, and here were white rednecks beating up black middle-class kids. The black leadership needed a record every day because nothing is worse than going out and being beaten up and having no media coverage. They wanted the whole country to witness what the real price of segregation was.

Martin King was a great tele-dramatist and understood it viscerally. Martin King, starting around '58 or '59, never went anywhere without his television crews, and he deliberately picked the worst cities because it was like throwing the other side a banana peel to slip on. He knew the more violently they responded to provocation, the more the American center would turn upon the segregationists.

Little Rock drew the line where each side learned how to maximize itself through the use of television. Orval Faubus stops the children from going to school, not because he's a racist, he does it largely because he wants to be re-elected. Arkansas is inhospitable to extra terms for its governor so he has nowhere to go. He draws the line and picks up the segregationists who have not necessarily been for him.

He learns, as does George Wallace, that if you get the Northern government and the courts and Feds angry at you it helps with the rednecks and the poor whites down South. On the other hand, Martin King was looking for a larger constituency and realizes if television shows poor whites beating up middle-class black kids who only want to get an education, the right to vote, or eat a Woolworth's hamburger, that the entire nation will gradually take the side of the ordinary black kid. So the political lines are drawn after Little Rock.

The one single event that changed the era was *Brown v. Board of Education* in 1954. The impact changed who we are in so many ways. You have to understand that before *Brown,* a black person growing up in Alabama or Mississippi not only had to go to an inferior school and have inferior service and ride on an inferior bus and generally be a second-class citizen, but he had to do this knowing it was mandated by the State.

After Brown, the State no longer said that he is *ipso facto* inferior. That's a profound moment.

CHAPTER 18

Integration in Little Rock

Harry Ashmore

On the evening of September 2, 1957, Governor Orval Faubus had the Arkansas National Guard establish a defensive zone around Central High School in Little Rock "to maintain order and prevent a riot." There was no violence planned. It was done to prevent ten black teenagers from attending classes.

A few weeks later, after much legal footwork, the students went to class. By this time, though, the situation had gotten out of hand, and troublemakers from around the state were looking for a fight. The mayor ordered the students withdrawn from school by noon that same day. The violence continued and the students stayed home. President Eisenhower called in the 101st Airborne, and the situation then calmed down. The students went back to Central High School.

It was a "black eye" for Little Rock and the country. Television had shown raw racism, and the country was appalled. It also revealed that racism was now going to be addressed by the government, and the less evident fact that the North, and the rest of the country, were going to experience their own racial problems in the near future.

The late Harry Ashmore was the executive editor of the *Arkansas Gazette* in Little Rock in 1957. He and the newspaper were awarded the first double Pulitzer Prizes for his editorials and the newspaper's coverage of the Little Rock integration crisis.

Little Rock was the first time raw racism appeared on television. Before that event, people only read about racial violence and confrontation. Now they were witnessing it and were appalled. Little Rock was a turning point in the Civil Rights Movement in America.

That's absolutely right. It was great television drama. Television had just become a national possibility. Before, it had been radio, but sound only couldn't get this, and print loses all the highly dramatic quality. The coaxial cable was coming in. You could receive television coast to coast. The television news crews were without any previous experience, so they were really experimenting with this. But, you're right, it put on home screens pictures of these defenseless black teenagers. All they were doing was demanding the rights the courts had already declared they had. It was a gruesome business.

The respectable whites were not involved in the mob action. They too were appalled by it. Many though were not willing to stand up and say so. Therefore the people on camera doing the attacking were the crackpots, who are always around. I once said that Orval Faubus had unlocked every looney bin in the South when he defied that court order. It certainly was shocking.

The *Brown* decision made possible the civil rights street demonstration because it committed the federal government, for the first time, to protect the rights of peaceful demonstrators against mobs or the local authorities who turned against them.

Before, either the police would have broken them up by force or simply would disappear and leave it to some civilian mob. The police would not act to control a mob where blacks were the victims. That suddenly ended. The federal government was now obligated to take over when that occurred. That meant Martin Luther King and his people could count on the fact that if they came up against real force, either organized or official, they could call for help and they'd get it. Eisenhower had to prove to Faubus he had more troops than Faubus did.

People who viewed this from afar on television believe to this day that they had a race riot in Little Rock so severe they had to send the U.S. Army to put it down. The fact is nobody at Little Rock was killed or even seriously injured . . . injured enough to be sent to the hospital.

There was never any semblance of a race riot. Nothing happened away from the school. Whites were not going into black neighborhoods nor [were] blacks pouring out. People still think this was an extremely violent scene. That's inherent in television. It depends on action. It wants controversy. It wants confrontation. It wants movement.

The city recovered fairly rapidly, and when the schools were closed the following year by Faubus, the whole city rallied and got the schools back open. They went into the most orderly desegregation that has taken place anywhere in the country. When the people recognized and accepted the fact that it was bad for business, that got the business community out. Chamber of Commerce-type leadership does not get into political controversy if it can possibly avoid it, but if it affects the pocket book, they move. When they move, of course, they've got the real clout. In every city in this country the property owners basically control the clout one way or another.

I don't say that critically. It's a capitalist-democracy and that's what makes the marigold. They couldn't stand the bad publicity and that galled. In addition, people's feelings were hurt in Little Rock. Proper people disapproved of the mob, felt they were being maligned, that they were being looked upon with contempt. Southerners have always had that feeling anyway, a sense of inferiority that's left over from the "lost war." So all that was exacerbated.

Television was a powerful influence and it was a mixed story, portraying what was happening there as a morality play with the usual roles reversed: A black being good and a white being evil. Very simplified terms. The white resistance was indefensible. I never thought there was any moral defense for segregation, but on the other hand, you're not going to change it until you begin to move politically.

When it was over, Faubus was still governor, but the city and the other urban places in Arkansas had turned against him. What grew out of that was a coalition of country club whites and black voters, because blacks were now voting fully. That finally led to Orval's defeat and ushered in all these moderate Democrats that now prevail across the South.

A great deal of good [came out of Little Rock]. It forced Eisenhower's hand and put this issue, for the first time, inescapably on the political agenda. It had to be dealt with. It also alerted the country, but they didn't pay enough attention to it, that this was no longer a unique Southern problem since the majority of blacks were no longer living in the South. The majority were now concentrated in the inner cities of the North, West and Midwest, and they were being ignored.

Nothing was being done about them and they were pouring in there, becoming this underclass that now represents the great urban problem of this country. In other words, this showdown reflected a demographic revolution that had taken place, not because of the mistreatment of blacks in the South, but because we'd mechanized agriculture, and these people of agrarian background had nowhere to go. So they'd gone north, not to escape Simon Legree, but to try to find something to eat.

CHAPTER 19

A Bitter Experience

Elizabeth Eckford

On a warm September day in 1957, Elizabeth Eckford went off to her first day of school. Nervous, wearing a new dress she and her sister had made, she hoped to make new friends. Instead, she was met with hatred, because Elizabeth was black and the school she was attempting to attend was Central High School in Little Rock, Arkansas.

Television for the first time revealed the ugliness of racism, leaving the country appalled and mortified. A famous photograph shows Elizabeth being screamed at by a white girl as she walks away from the school.

Elizabeth was one of ten black teenagers attempting to enter Central High School that day. Eventually nine were permitted to attend—one girl dropped out—but not without paying a terrible psychological price. Both black and white owe Elizabeth and her fellow black students a debt of gratitude for showing the stupidity and ugliness of racial hatred.

It was an ordinary day and an extraordinary day. It was to have been my first day at a new school, but my routine that day was the same as it would have been for any first day in school. I was wearing a new dress that my sister and I had made. I was thinking that I didn't know who my teachers were going to be. I didn't know how the students would react to me. Would I make any friends?

I knew that some of my neighbors were students at Central, so I expected to see some familiar faces. But I did not have any friends there, and I wasn't sure who among the Negro students would be going, because prior to that time we had had meetings with the school superintendent, along with our families. But we were not a group prior to that time. These were individuals, acting individually.

I took the city bus a few blocks from my house and rode to within two blocks of the school. I got off the bus at the regular stop, and I noticed there were more cars than usual parked along the street. See, I had passed Central High School regularly. It was on my way to the junior high school, and later the senior high school that I attended. Also, it was the path going to my grandfather's store, so the surroundings were very familiar to me.

Walking up the street I could hear the murmur of the crowd, but I felt reassured knowing that the National Guard was going to be there. The National Guard were stationed around the grounds of the school.

They got quiet as they became aware of me. I made three attempts to get on the school grounds. I was barred three times [by the Guard], and the third time I was directed across the street, where the crowd of people were. Later the newspaper estimated there were about 350 people in that crowd.

They began to shout ugly things, and when I stepped out in the street they surged toward me. I had to change directions and go forward to 16th Street where I knew there would be another bus stop. The National Guard was never "with" me. The National Guard, the soldiers, were lined up in front of the school and all along the school grounds. It was after I stepped out onto the street and the people surged forward [that they] started calling me names and screaming other things. They were behind me. Photographers, and I guess reporters, were directly in front of me.

I tried to concentrate on getting to the bus stop, and when I got to that corner I realized there was a drugstore across the street. I tried to get there to call a cab, and as I got to the door the proprietor locked the door. I went back to the bench and waited for the bus.

It took some time before it came; the bus was practically empty. There was a white woman. All the reporters in their stories afterwards interpreted her presence as being there to help me. This woman engaged the mob and got on the bus with me, but I was able to persuade her after about four blocks, after the bus had crossed the bridge, that I didn't need her help, and she got off the bus. I went directly to the Negro Deaf & Blind School, where my mother was, just a few blocks from my home.

This was September 4. We didn't get into school until September 23rd. We were in school for a couple of hours on September 23rd before the police had to remove us because there were 1,000 people out front, and when they found we were in school they tried to overrun the police lines. Some of the policemen threw down their badges rather than confront their own people. President Eisenhower sent the 101st Airborne Division on the night of the 24th, and we were taken in by them on the 25th.

The Arkansas National Guard was federalized over the 101st. Actually, the 101st was only in the school for three weeks and then their presence diminished, though they were still in town. Their orders were to observe and report, not to intercede. They only guarded us in the hallway. They didn't go into the classrooms or into the auditorium or to the playing field. The majority of the attacks on us were in the hallways or in the shower room in the gym.

We eventually were able to identify a core of about fifty-five people who were organized, who were our regular attackers, but the majority of people simply turned away, pretended they didn't hear and didn't see [us]. At first there were several overtures of friendliness, but [that] very quickly dissipated. They were very easily and very quickly intimidated.

Among the nine of us [a female had now dropped out], we could identify about ten people who were consistently friendly or tried to treat us like everybody else.

How were they treated by the other white kids?

They were attacked. They got nasty phone calls and one guy was punched out. He was a senior, and he graduated with Ernest (one of the nine black students). There's a photograph of him standing near Ernest and other students in the background. The photograph was taken on Ernest's graduation day.

We were [in] all classes. Ernest was the only senior. The rest were sophomores or juniors. I was a junior. At that time Central was only tenth, eleventh and twelfth grades. Now, it is ninth, tenth, eleventh, and twelfth [with] elementary, middle school, and high school. At that time it had elementary, junior high, and high school.

All the high schools in Little Rock were closed in 1958. There was a group of women called "The Women's Emergency Committee." After a long, long campaign [they got the high schools opened]. They found out what it was like to be treated like Negroes. Their phones were tapped. They got intimidating phone calls. Their husbands' jobs were in jeopardy.

The legislature passed a series of segregationist laws giving towns the option of opening all of their schools on a desegregated basis or closing some of the schools. The majority of the voters in Little Rock voted to close the schools rather than have all the high schools opened on a desegregated basis. They reopened in August of '59.

During the year the high schools were closed, I took correspondence courses. There were high school courses, the majority of them from the University of Arkansas at Fayetteville, and a French course from the University of Missouri. During the summer of '59, those of us who had remained here were shipped across the country, where people took us in voluntarily and we went to summer school in those towns. I went to St. Louis.

Of the original group, only two came back when the schools were reopened—Carlotta Walls and Jefferson Thomas. Some of the others' families lost their livelihood and had to move from Little Rock. I went on to college. I didn't finish high school, but I went on to college. I got enough credits to be admitted to college, but I didn't graduate from high school. I went to Knox College in Galesburg, Illinois. I went there one year. Eventually, I graduated, but many, many years later.

I'm at the point now where I'm able to talk about it. But my experiences were no different from the rest, except for that first day.

It was the first time the federal government and the executive branch acted to enforce court orders—the court desegregation orders. [It was] the first time Eisenhower ever acted, because this had happened in Marshall, Texas, and Clinton, Tennessee. Mobs had turned back attempts to desegregate. In Texas, the governor called out the state police to enforce mob rule.

The president hadn't acted [before] so Little Rock was different in that respect, and also it was different because those photographs were published worldwide and there was an international reaction. Somebody threatened to take the case to the United Nations on humanitarian grounds. This was the time of the Cold War. It was good propaganda for the communists. This was the first time something like this was covered by television so people saw things as they happened. That was unique.

I think about the images of the Civil Rights Movement, and I know economic pressure was brought to bear on some communities where these ugly images showed up. Businesses didn't want to move into those places. But I don't think the [local] people were ashamed. I think [they were] more affected by the economic impact than anything else.

It was a grudging acceptance that they had to follow the rule of law. The school board actively fought to delay desegregation. Initially it was supposed to be just a token plan. What are nine Negro students but tokens?

CHAPTER 20

My Life Is More Than One Moment

Hazel Bryan Massery

In one of history's most famous photographs, Hazel, as a fifteen-year-old high school junior, is seen screaming at Elizabeth Eckford as she departs Central High School in Little Rock, Arkansas, after being refused admission by the Arkansas National Guard in September 1957.

In 1963 Hazel emotionally called Elizabeth and apologized. She had come to realize the hurt and wrong she had done and made amends. Still living in Little Rock, she is a great-grandmother and has been married for forty-two years.

I don't remember [everything]. I was fifteen years old, a junior in high school. I realized something unusual was happening. The excitement of starting back to school with new clothes, the usual excitement of a typical teenager, then additionally knowing from adults talking, newspapers, and television that this is not a normal beginning of school, that something was in the air.

We didn't know quite what to expect. I had not met with many students up until that time, but television and the governor feared there was going to be trouble and violence.

Elizabeth [Eckford] and I did some speaking [together] for a while, but I decided I wasn't going to do that anymore. I've been trying to forget this. I said if anybody called it was "I have no comment." I don't know why I told you I would do this. I've been trying to put it out of my mind and just go on with my life in the present.

School used to start the day after Labor Day, on a Tuesday. When we got to school, the National Guard was around the school, and there was a lot of media. This was something new. It was among the first large events to be covered by television.

Central is a large school. Elizabeth had tried to enter at the other end of the school and the Guard wouldn't let her. She knew there was a bus stop at the other end and was trying to get to the bus stop. There was a crowd in front and people started jeering her. I was probably three-quarters of the way down with a friend, and by the time she got there they were following her and jeering her, and I joined in the crowd.

This was pretty exciting, a new experience with all the reporters and television. I didn't realize the seriousness of it, the impact it would have on other people. I was in front of the cameras. The cameras were rolling, and I wanted to show-off.

My friend's father started yelling at her, and in the picture you will see a girl with her head turned. He started yelling at us to stop, to get out of that . . . it could lead to violence. It could have gotten dangerous. Nobody knew what was going on so he was yelling at us to stop. So we stopped.

We skipped school. I think we went to my friend's house not far away. There were several of us that walked on to her house.

[With the famous picture] there was a mixture of the attention I was getting, but underneath [I was] seeing [myself] do this to another person. A lot of confusion on everybody's part for the social changes that were taking place, and you couldn't grasp what was happening, what was going to happen.

Kids I talk to today cannot comprehend the limited contact we had with blacks or even seeing black people. They were sort of in the background. The only black people I ever saw were the black men who came to pick up our garbage once a week. Occasionally when you went to town you might see some that would move out of your way when you passed by. The social change that was happening, I mean, you're just in a state of confusion. *You have your schools. Why do you want to go to school with us?*

I don't remember anybody saying much of anything about the picture. I only went to Central about a week. My parents were afraid I might be in danger, especially my mother. We have city and county schools, and we lived closer to a county school than to Central, but I was in the city limits. My mother got me out of Central and into the county school in about a week.

I met my husband the first day I was signing in at the new school. My sister was two grades behind me, and we both were sent to this school and were signing in and my sister nudged me—the guys came around to look at the new girls that were signing in.

She said, "Take a look at that one."

I looked at him and said, "Hands off. That one's mine." And we've been married forty-two years.

Somebody asked him [about the picture], "What were you doing?" And he said, "I was slopping the hogs."

I had letters sent to me. I remember the girl's vice-principal at Central, Miss Huckleby, calling me into the office to give me these letters that were from out of state. I read those letters and they all said what I did was wrong. This was my first encounter with anybody white having another perspective on it. I didn't know anyone who had a different perspective, who wanted desegregation, who felt that was what needed to be done.

When you talk to people that were in our class, they have this resentment that our school year was ruined. That year was so tumultuous with the Guard there. I have a letter from one of the guys that he wrote years later explaining he had nightmares about the Guard being in Central and he couldn't get out. The blacks think that this just impacted their lives, and I know it was bad, really bad. But it did impact other people's lives, too. People thought, *They're teenagers, they're big kids.* But it did [have impact].

In 1963 I was married, was a young mother, had two very small children. Television was covering the civil rights movement and I was seeing people fire hosed and the dogs. There were things going on in Birmingham, and [Alabama Gov. George] Wallace had his school stand, and there was the march on Washington in August. Also, the Birmingham bombing of the school—those three little girls killed. And it also happened to be the centennial of the Emancipation Proclamation.

Probably all of this had some impact on my thinking about what it was like to be black, what they had gone through, and what it must have felt like. Turn it around. What if that had been me? How would I have felt, putting myself in her place?

I called Elizabeth in September 1963 and apologized. She wasn't living here. She was just home by coincidence. I told her who I was and that I was sorry. I was emotional at the time and crying, and she asked me about my life, and I told her I was married and I had two little boys. We didn't talk very long.

I never met Elizabeth until the '97 commemoration. Little Rock had a big forty-year commemoration [for the Central High School Visitors Center] in September '97. The president was here and made a speech. While here for the commemoration, people were calling to interview me and Will Counts.

Will Counts is the man who shot that picture in '57. He was a local person. He was not in a suit and tie like the guys from New York, so he was thought of as just a person out there taking pictures. He got by, although there was some opposition to people taking pictures.

A person who knew me approached him the day the visitor's center was opened and asked him if he ever thought about taking another picture of us. He said, "Well, yes, but nobody knows who the other girl is."

She said, "I do, and I have her phone number."

She called me and asked would I like to speak to Will and if I wanted another picture. I said I'd be elated to. He talked to Elizabeth and she did too, and he got us together and had another picture taken. That was on the front page of the paper, I think September 23, 1997. There was a lot of publicity over that. Then people asked us to do speeches and we did that for about three and a half years.

Seeing the racial violence on TV certainly impacted my thinking. Seeing pictures like that, I suppose there is some good to the media. It just makes you think. When you just hear about it, you don't see it, but when you see somebody mistreated like that . . .

How is the racial situation in Arkansas now?

A lot better. It's not perfect by any means, but from forty years ago—certainly, certainly. Economically there is a difference, but there's definitely been an improvement.

I was interviewed in '97 and the reporter wanted a quote. I asked her what she wanted. She said, "Well, just keep talking. I'll find something."

I went on talking, like I'm talking to you, and I said, "Well, my life is more than that one moment."

She said, "That's it. Can I quote that?"

I said, "Please do."

When Will Counts heard that, he was really taken, because he was always taught as a photo-journalist to capture the moment. He wrote a book, and the name of it is *Life Is More Than One Moment.* He went back to Central and took pictures showing the difference forty years makes—the blacks and the whites together.

CHAPTER 21

Rock and Roll

Steve Goddard

Musical tastes in America during the early- to mid-1950s were unique in that adults and young people basically liked the same music. Artists such as Frankie Laine, Rosemary Clooney, Perry Como, The Hilltoppers, and Jo Stafford were enjoyed by a broad demographic group.

In 1955 Bill Haley's "Rock Around The Clock" changed that. Rock and roll became a monster, and though many believed it would be a passing fad, Elvis, Little Richard, Chuck Berry, Fats Domino, and others made it a world-wide phenomenon.

Steve Goddard has been a top-rated disc jockey for over thirty years, working in Dallas, San Diego, Phoenix, and Oklahoma City. He is a student of the early days of rock and roll and has a syndicated "oldies" show called Goddard's Gold.

If you were to pick a watershed year it is 1955, because it gave us *"Rock Around the Clock,"* which had been released the year earlier and had done absolutely nothing. Then it was featured in *The Blackboard Jungle,* and by July '55 it was number one—probably the first legitimate number one rock and roll record. Music had turned the corner.

You can go back to 1948 for Roy Brown, who did *"Good Rockin' Tonight,"* which Elvis would later re-record for Sun Records. The Ravens had a track called *"Rock All Night Long"* that same year. Fats Domino had *"The Fat Man"* in 1950, which some people consider to be the first rock and roll record. *"Sixty Minute Man"* by The Dominos can be traced to 1951.

Jackie Brenston had a number one rhythm and blues hit with *"Rocket 88,"* which Bill Haley covered in 1951. Bill also recorded *"Rock the Joint"* in late 1951 and *"Crazy Man Crazy"* in 1953, which preceded *"Rock Around The Clock"* by over a year. *"Ting-a-Ling"* by The Clovers you can trace to '52. So '55 was the beginning, the explosion that had been building up in the years previous.

Nineteen fifty-five was the last gasp for many artists. You had Nat "King" Cole having hits into the late fifties, and Perry Como was still hanging on the charts. But for Frankie Laine and artists of that type, it knocked them for a loop. Frankie Laine never had a Top Twenty hit after May 1957. Aside from one Top Ten single in June 1958, Doris Day never had a single reach higher than forty-two on the Hot 100 charts.

That compares with eighteen Top Twenty hits between 1950 and 1955. And ironically enough, the biggest record of '55, according to Joel Whitburn, was not *"Rock Around The Clock,"* but *"Cherry Pink and Apple Blossom White"* by Perez Prado, which certainly wouldn't have happened in '56 when Elvis took over.

By 1956 Sam Phillips had recorded Elvis, Carl Perkins, and Johnny Cash. [In] '56 RCA recorded Elvis for the first time, and we haven't really recovered since. That was probably Bill Haley's peak year. He was making all those horrible rock and roll movies with Alan Freed.

Carl Perkins broke through with *"Blue Suede Shoes."* Fats Domino had finally crossed over. Pat Boone still had a few hits with cover songs, but for the most part people wanted to hear the real thing.

It was either John Lennon or Buddy Holly who said, "Without Elvis, none of us would have made it." Elvis was the role model. If not Elvis, someone would have done it. It wouldn't have happened the same way, possibly without the same impact, but it would have happened.

You remember '55, '56, '57, before Elvis went into the army, Elvis was the standard for cool. He borrowed from Tony Curtis, and he liked some Dean Martin ballads, and he liked James Dean. People borrowed from Elvis. Elvis borrowed from a lot of other people, black and white artists.

Ironically enough, a lot of black artists didn't change their style at all when rock and roll hit. Everyone else caught up to them. Big Joe Turner had been shouting jump blues since the late forties, early fifties. Later he would tour with Bill Haley. Fats Domino didn't appreciably change his style. They were played on the "race" radio stations. The white kids would tune these in because it was a hell of a lot more exciting to hear these guys sing the songs than the white cover versions by Pat Boone and Georgia Gibbs.

I spoke with Pat Boone a number of years ago. He wasn't defensive, but put it in perspective, "Look, I helped open the door for these guys." Little Richard has gone so far as to say if Pat Boone hadn't covered some of his songs, and the white audience hadn't heard Pat Boone's versions and then been curious as to what the original sounded like, he might not have happened.

Everybody thought rock and roll was going to fade. I've heard interviews with Elvis and Buddy Holly, and they were always asked, "What are you going to do when it goes away?" Nobody had any idea. They were thinking of rock and roll as a temporary fad.

Elvis half kiddingly commented on several occasions that if it all ended today he'd go back to driving a truck! (Which he had done for Crown Electric in Memphis—even after being signed by Sun Records!)

The only way I can explain it is, once you've heard Jerry Lee Lewis, Little Richard, and Elvis in their prime, it's pretty tough to go back to Joni James, Frankie Laine, and Johnny Ray. And also, every generation that comes along . . . the kids have to have their own music. It happened with Elvis. It happened with The Beatles. It's happened with rap music today. Kids love it because the parents hate it.

I had a little record player and I had all the Little Richard records. I used to wait for that scream . . . the inevitable scream before the sax solo, about a third or half way through the song.

They always had a verse or two, chorus, and then a scream, and then a sax solo. I just loved that. I drove my parents crazy with it. I wore out a 78 of "Rock Around The Clock." I wore out several 45s. I remember on Sundays it was unspoken . . . we don't play rock and roll on Sundays, but if we do, we turn down the volume.

There's a video clip of Rev. Jimmy Snow denouncing rock and roll, saying, "What is it the kids like about rock and roll? The beat. The beat. The beat."

And yeah, it was the beat. You know, it was exciting.

Dick Clark was the most powerful man in rock and roll because he had a national show. Dick Clark was squeaky clean, and parents could accept Dick Clark more than they could Alan Freed. Alan Freed was a lot rawer. Dick Clark was polished and just kind of nice. He's easy going and made the parents feel comfortable. They also were opposite in appearance. Alan Freed looked a little seedy. Dick Clark looked like he'd never had a speck of dirt touch him. Never an overly "Brylcreamed" hair out of place.

The biggest single individual who made rock and roll palatable for parents was Ricky Nelson. Ricky started to sing on the television show in '57. They got a lot of letters and lot of flack from parents about "how could you let your kid sing this rock and roll?"

Ozzie and Harriet did some shows on the acceptance of rock and roll. I remember one scene where Rick comes in and asks Harriet, "What do you think about rock and roll?"

And she says, "Well, we're pretty brainwashed by now, but at least I can stay in the same room with it."

Ricky would always sing a song at the end of the show, and that exposure and acceptance by Ozzie and Harriet broke down a lot of barriers for parents.

Little Richard was the least acceptable to parents. Right off the bat. He was a wild man. He was a black wild man. He was crazy. But I'll go you one further than Little Richard. There was a fellow named Esquerita who makes Little Richard sound very polished, and Richard took some things from him.

Esquerita did one album for Capitol, and I have no idea why they would record it because I can't believe anybody would have thought it would have sold. It is so raw, but it's great. Jerry Lee Lewis was another, after everybody found out he'd married his cousin.

CHAPTER 22

Splendored, but Brief

Al Alberts

Al Alberts was the lead singer of The Four Aces, one of America's favorite singing groups in the early 1950s, dominating the charts with such hits as "It's No Sin," "Stranger In Paradise," "Three Coins In The Fountain," and "Love Is A Many-Splendored Thing."

By 1957 rock and roll was firmly entrenched and their style of music was no longer popular. Rock and roll was on Al before he knew it, and he left The Four Aces in 1958 to perform as a single. He harbors no bitterness; he was a star for longer than most.

Ironically, the other three members of The Four Aces were from Chester, Pennsylvania, and were friends of Bill Haley, also from Chester. Bill Haley's "Rock Around The Clock" changed music forever, effectively ending The Four Aces' careers.

You're so involved in the experience that you don't realize what's happening. Looking back now, when you go from date to date, recording to recording, and television show to television show, you're so preoccupied with what you have to do that you're really not thoroughly enjoying the experience.

I look back at it now with great satisfaction, but while it's happening you're just too involved looking for that next recording 'cause you've gotta follow up a "Written On The Wind," you gotta follow up a "Three Coins In The Fountain."

You get two days off and your manager puts you on "The Ed Sullivan Show." You very seldom get a chance to see your family, and it's just an ongoing experience without too much time to sit back and say, "Hey, this is really fun." While it's happening I don't think too many performers really feel it's fun. It's hard work. We were on the road an average of forty-five weeks a year.

I never gave rock and roll serious consideration, and I'm sure many of the other guys in our trade felt the same. Everybody expected it to be a quick fad because music needs that constant change. Nobody expected it to hang in there. The first rock and roll recordings, such as Bill Haley's *"Rock Around The Clock"* and *"Shake, Rattle and Roll,"* you could actually sing the melodies. The shape rock and roll took afterwards no one foresaw, with acid rock, then hard metal, which to me is strictly junk.

I was always so intent on the structure of The Four Aces that I never thought that rock and roll would affect the top entertainers in the business, and we were considered number one in the world at that time.

When I left, rock and roll really took over, which I had not anticipated. When it went to acid and to metal, I was even more determined that it would not last because it was junk. People would not buy it, but they did.

I resented acid and metal because of the effect it had on our kids. It led to the dope scene. It led to kids drinking at thirteen and fourteen years of age because they saw pictures of their stars bombed out of their skulls.

I always had a total positive approach to my business. I never discussed rock and roll with other members of the trade because they would think that I was complaining, that my career wasn't happening.

The idea is to make the world believe, *Hey, man, I left and I'm swinging and I'm traveling around the world.* After I left The Aces, my market basically was the Orient and Europe. I traveled that market literally six months a year, every year, for ten years. Japan, Okinawa, Taiwan, Bangkok, Singapore . . . you name it, we were there.

We had a lot of military bases in those areas. The bottom line was go over for the military on a three-month deal, and then maybe ten days to two weeks out of that contract period we would be working the local economy. As the military phased out, we literally moved to the local economy, because my ticket to the Orient was *"Love Is A Many-Splendored Thing."*

I honestly believe that we lived through the most beautiful decade the world has known in the fifties. Music-wise, for sure. I look back at it now . . . I look at some of the photos. MCA called me for information to release our first CD with them. They've packaged eighteen of our major recordings, and they needed pictures and any tidbits.

It forced me to go back to our scrapbook and the pictures we took on tour and the reviews that we had around the world. It brought back so many great memories. I've always looked back on that period with a sweet taste in my mouth. It was a great, great era. I look back at that period of time as the greatest ten years of my life. I'll never forget it.

Every city we went to, we knew every disc jockey, from the number one man down to the overnight man. We knew their wives, the names of their kids, what their hobbies were. Every time we went in we had luncheons with all these guys. We knew the names of the juke box operators in those cities. When we had time we visited the major record stores and talked to the gals behind the counter.

In fact, our recording of *"Heart Of My Heart,"* which was a million-seller, was recommended to me during a meeting in a record store in Chicago. The girl behind the counter said, "Al, there's one song people come in and ask about 'cause they're having a party, blah, blah, blah, blah . . . and there's really no good recording of *'Heart Of My Heart.'* Why don't you do the recording?"

So when we came up for *"Three Coins In The Fountain"* we needed a B-side, and that was the B-side.

We felt an obligation to the kids who were buying our records. We tried to set a precedent. We wanted to be a role model for them, and I honestly think we succeeded. The thing I resent today is that some of the major entertainers, and I use that word very loosely—entertainers—are still role models to the kids. But they're the wrong role models, between the dope and the booze scene. How you change that, I don't know. But it won't change until the face of music changes again.

CHAPTER 23

Memories

Jimmy Sacca

Post-war music was primarily romantic and sentimental. Some
examples:

Perry Como	*"No Other Love"*
	"Wanted"
Rosemary Clooney	*"Tenderly"*
	"Hey There"
The Four Aces	*"Stranger in Paradise"*
	"Love Is A Many Splendored Thing"
The Hilltoppers	*"Trying"*
	"P. S. I Love You"
Joni James	*"Why Don't You Believe Me?"*
	"Have You Heard?"
Kitty Kallen	*"Little Things Mean A Lot"*
	"In The Chapel In The Moonlight"

Today you seldom hear the music of these artists. For the
most part they were history by the late fifties, buried by rock
and roll. As one of The Hilltopper's songs laments, *"Time Waits
For No One."*

Jimmy Sacca was the lead singer for The Hilltoppers. Rock
and roll ruined more than peace and quiet.

Dick Clark, back in the early fifties, depended on groups like The
Four Aces, The Hilltoppers, The Ames Brothers, The Four Lads, The
Crew Cuts. All these great groups of the fifties. Now for some reason
or other they're never mentioned. This hurts me more than rock and
roll coming in and taking over. That really didn't bother me because
there's plenty of room for all kinds of music. But I'll never know what
happened to the groups of the fifties.

These people played a big, big part in the lives of a lot of people. You'd be amazed how many letters I got from men and women who were in the Korean War, saying they got solace in our music such as "P.S. I Love You." That's how they would sign off when they were writing letters.

All the years I was on the road people would come up and ask, "Jimmy, why are you still knocking yourself out on the road?" I'd tell them we played a part in so many people's lives that I wanted to be out there and maybe bring back a memory or two. But the good singers of the early fifties have just been forgotten. This hurts not only me, but I'm sure it hurts the other groups.

Those groups led the way for your rock and roll groups. Listen to the groups of the early fifties, the styles. There was a lead singer with three voices backing up, doing the "oohs" and the "aahs." What were The Platters? Same thing.

There's a book that shows all the songs that have been on the charts from 1890. I looked through the book to see the groups that had the most songs on the charts, in the Top 100, over that period of time, and it's amazing. I think The Four Aces were like sixth or eighth. The Mills Brothers were there. Our group was twenty-sixth. All the groups [were there], including Mick Jagger, The Beatles, The Animals, all of them. So twenty-sixth was a pretty good position.

We put out a record and both sides would hit. "P.S. I Love You" got up to number three in the nation. Then, when it started coming down, the other side, "I'd Rather Die Young," hit the Top Ten.

We did that for I don't know how many years. "Till Then" came out, got on the charts, and the other side—"To Be Alone"—then got in the Top Ten.

I loved it. That's the only memories I've got. I loved it all. I love being home with my family, too, but you can't have your cake and eat it too. I was happy in those years. I enjoyed entertaining, I knew I was making people happy.

I reminisce a lot when I hear old songs, but I don't go to bed and worry about it. I'd love to get my youth back again, as everybody would. I know it's impossible to go back. I reminisce a lot when I talk to somebody like you.

The only regret I've got is the service really took the best years of my life. When I went in the service in February '53, "P.S. I Love You" just came out. The only regret I have is that I couldn't cash in on the really big dollars that were out at the time because the service held me back.

The transition to rock and roll came from 1953 to '55, when I was overseas. Before I went overseas, we recorded songs. During the year to come the music started to change and those songs didn't fit. I wasn't released from the service until mid-1955, and when I got out, two of the other guys went in.

That's where my regrets are. We could have proved we had the ability to move into the rock and roll era, but being overseas in Korea and Okinawa, they didn't have any recording studios. That put us back more than anything.

I'm living with it. I'm with my wife, and I've got beautiful children and grandchildren. I'm happy, but when the subject comes up, I get upset.

PART III

The Last Hurrah

(Edwin O'Connor)

CHAPTER 24

The 1960s

Roger Kimball

Roger Kimball, author of *The Long March: How the Cultural Revolution of the 1960s Changed America,* believes more than a residue of the sixties remains in the present culture. He contends that once unleashed upon the public, "sixtyism"—with its lack of personal responsibility, self-absorption, prolonged adolescence, and unique versions of history—has resisted being sent to St. Helena.

One of the myths of the sixties is that the fifties was not only a care-taker decade, but a decade of intellectual conformity, political quies-cence, and spiritual torpor. That is a total misrepresentation of the decade. In comparison to what came after it, the 1950s looks more or less like fifth-century Athens.

The country had just fought and won a world war. It was economi-cally dynamic, politically respected the world over. Intellectually, it had been bolstered by a lot of immigrant talent from Europe that had come here to escape Hitler. Artistically, there were poets like T. S. Eliot, Wallace Stevens, Robert Frost. It was a time when Balanchine was just getting the New York City Ballet together. Artistically, intel-lectually, socially it was exciting, but still tradition minded.

It was a time when many social injustices were beginning to be faced up to. The birth of the Civil Rights Movement has to be traced to the fifties, and many things that were inequitable in our society were being addressed in a gradualist, rational way. All that gave way in the sixties to the black power movements, and so on.

The fifties was the last decade of a common culture in which moral, intellectual, and artistic standards were widely agreed upon and upheld. The charge that the 1950s was a sterile and politically conformist and intellectually shallow decade is a total misrepresentation of the truth.

The Kennedy assassination was a catalyst—one among many catalysts—but it did not cause the sixties. It certainly was a cataclysmic event in the culture, but we would have had the sixties anyway. My own view is we saw mainstreaming, a kind of institutionalization of various radical elements that had been articulated earlier. Intellectually some of them went back to Rousseau and some of the avant-garde figures of the French nineteenth century.

I think the jazz age of the 1920s represented an immoralist current that was cut off by the Depression, then World War II. The beat generation of Allen Ginsberg and William Burroughs [was] on the fringe when they first emerged into public consciousness, but within a few years their whole menu of radical sentiment—the anti-Americanism, the sexual promiscuity, the celebration of drugs as a root to higher consciousness, the narcissism, the hedonism, the whole menu of what would later turn out to characterize large parts of our culture— were articulated by these beat figures, and what we saw as the sixties was the acceptance of these sentiments into mainstream society. Sentiments that hitherto would have been confined to a tiny fringe without much institutional power or influence.

We saw a capitulation on the part of the old-style liberal establishment to a moral antinomianism that took place increasingly as the sixties wore on. With the Vietnam War, it got a big shot in the arm, and with the concelebration of the unholy trinity of sex, drugs, and rock and roll, it really installed itself at the center of American culture.

As we moved into the seventies, mainstream society, which had mounted considerable resistance to these forces, began to accommodate itself to these new radical sentiments. A good example is what happened in the art world. Up through the time of the abstract expressionists there was still a great deal of resistance to the avant-garde in art. It used to be that you could count upon the man on the street to resist some of the wilder things perpetrated by the so-called avant-garde.

Now the man on the street began to celebrate it. There was no resistance whatsoever. Any new fad that came down the pipe was instantly celebrated as the next work of genius. The same thing happened in the world of manners and morals. You saw an entire culture embrace the most far-out attitudes toward life and accept them in the way people dressed. Blue jeans at one point was a badge of the counter-culture.

At some point in the seventies everyone began wearing blue jeans. It might seem insignificant, but this sartorial badge once reserved for the counter-culture actually betokens a great change in our attitudes toward manners and social life in general.

The same with drugs, sex, and rock and roll. As things became more and more commercially successful, and more and more widespread, people lost their resistance. There was a spiritual immune system that became compromised by the onslaught.

I think it is impossible to isolate any one cause or set of causes for any historical event. It's just too complex. People are still debating what the cause of the First World War was. When it comes to the cultural revolution, one can point to a number of things. Things like greater affluence, greater mobility, the perfection of contraceptions, television, the dissemination of rock and roll, tranquilizers.

There were a lot of things that came together in the late fifties that softened up the culture and made it receptive to these ideas. Indeed, one important cause [was] the characters I talk about in my book *The Long March*. People like Norman Mailer, Susan Sontag, and Eldridge Cleaver and institutions like the *New York Review of Books*.

[Bill] Clinton was the first baby-boomer president. The first counter-cultural president. The first, you might say, post-modern president. I remember vividly when the Monica Lewinsky affair first broke, watching a television program in which a number of talking heads, pundits from both sides, said, "Well, if this is true, we will measure the Clinton presidency in a matter of days, not months or years."

Well, of course, it did not turn out to be true, and this moral pigmy continued to occupy the highest office in the land. The response was indifference to moral enormity on the one hand, and exasperation with President Clinton's critics for calling attention to the problem.

We have now interpreted freedom of religion to mean freedom from religion. Thirty or forty years ago that would never had been countenanced. The Brooklyn Museum had an exhibition not long ago which caused a great outcry called Sensations. It consisted of ridiculous figures from Britain, and the real cause célèbre was a picture of the Virgin Mary covered with pornographic pictures and clumps of elephant dung.

The ACLU, and all those so-called First Amendment fanatics, along with the so-called arts community, rushed to the defense of the Brooklyn Museum and talked about artistic freedom and the First Amendment. What would have happened had the Brooklyn Museum had a crèche at Christmas time with statutes of the Holy Family, including the Virgin Mary? The ACLU would have been on them in a flash talking about the separation of church and state.

Another big change is the attitude toward sexuality. Herbert Marcuse, the Marxist Frankfurt School philosopher, wrote a very influential book called *Era of Civilization,* which is a blending of a radical view of Marx and a radical view of Freud. He thought a kind of polymorphous sexuality was the answer to all of our problems, and [that] we should emancipate sexuality from procreation and understand that sexuality was really just a means of entertaining ourselves.

He wanted people to encourage the narcissist in themselves and view sexuality as a means of self-gratification, quite apart from the family.

He was an immensely influential figure, and his gospel had a huge impact. He wasn't the only one preaching free love, but he was one of the most influential. What we see today is the result of Marcuse's views. The idea all human beings are an amorphous bundle of sexual craving that should be gratified at every instant without any thought to the moral consequences has always been part of the counter-cultural movement. You see it on network television, on billboards, and in magazines. The culture is really obsessed with it, and it was inconceivable thirty years ago.

[Lyndon] Johnson's Great Society programs helped to foster welfare cultural dependence that has only gotten worse and worse. President Nixon, while widely excoriated at the time, was actually a very liberal president and instituted measures from wage and price controls to beefing up the budget for the National Endowment for the Arts. He in his own way, almost as much as Lyndon Johnson, fostered a welfare society in which the individual was encouraged to look to the state rather than to his own resources to get on in life.

In de Tocqueville's book *Democracy in America,* he states despotism will come to democratic societies not by tyrannizing the populace, but by infantilizing it through the proliferation of evermore onerous rules and regulations that we thread into the fabric of daily life. You see that everywhere around us, the state becoming more and more powerful.

Chief Justice Marshall said that the power to tax is the power to destroy; just look at what's happened to taxes over the last several decades. The government gets larger and larger and more and more paternalistic. We have creeping nanny state-ism that certainly would have been abominated thirty or forty years ago.

The turning point for things going wrong is the decade of the sixties. The assault on intellectual standards. The assault on moral standards. The erosion of personal responsibility. The celebration of the welfare state and cultural dependency. The demonization of America. All of these things unfolded over a period of time. Things were a lot different in the summer of 1958 than the summer of 1965.

Why? It was partly the Vietnam War. It was partly the institutionalization of rock music with its gospel of sexual excess and drugs. It was the so-called Woodstock generation, the Age of Aquarius. What had once been confined to a tiny fringe of society suddenly became part and parcel of what affluent people were doing all over the country. It was a triumph of prolonged adolescence. Everyone of whatever age reverted to adolescence.

Will the sixties ever end?

That's a good question. Things have gotten to such a state in our culture that there's now a reaction. I live in a little community where many are parents of young children, and most of the people are politically liberal, but they're terrified of the schools. Not only because of the intellectual problems with the dummying down, the political correctness, and so on, but the moral assault. The idea that representatives from the latest gay activist group are given equal time, indeed if not more time, than those of tradition-minded values. We're in a situation where many of the social institutions which we used to look to to preserve and transmit traditional culture are now bent on destroying them.

Hillary Clinton talks about it in *It Takes A Village*. She wants to hand over the education of the nation's children to a liberal leaf like herself. She wants to make it impossible for parents to bring up their children to be God- fearing, upright citizens. Even to use the word *God-fearing* now in many circumstances, you have to almost put quotation marks around it. That is a gigantic change from thirty or forty years ago.

Why have parents ceded so much authority and control to institutions that truly are inimical to everything they believe in, from their attitude toward the United States to religion to sexual morality to intellectual standards—right down the line? Many schools and colleges are committed to undoing the culture that parents have spent years trying to instill in their children.

There is beginning to be a response to the excesses our culture has embraced. The country has devoted itself to greater and greater accumulation and consumption, which is welcomed by both liberals and some conservatives these days. This confusion of the moral good with material affluence is bound to be challenged by reality sooner or later.

The world is a very dangerous place. We have been very lucky in this country. We're very rich. We're very powerful in military and economic terms. But we have a lot of enemies, and I think the next time there's a crisis, as there are always crises in the life of a society, I believe people will find the values they embraced in the fifties and sixties will not serve them well. I suspect there will be a great deal of soul searching and reaction against the excesses of the so-called purple decade.

CHAPTER 25

The Cuban Missile Crisis

Dino Brugioni

Dino Brugioni is one of America's unsung heroes. As a senior
official in reconnaissance and photo interpretation at the
Central Intelligence Agency, he helped discover missiles in Cuba
in August 1962.

All during the summer of 1962 the Russians began sending more and
more military equipment to Cuba. It was under the most careful aerial surveillance. On August 29, 1962, we found surface-to-air missiles.
Mr. [John] McCone [CIA director] said, "They're not putting the surface-to-air missiles in to protect the cane cutters. They're putting
them in to blind our reconnaissance eye."

The finding of the surface-to-air missiles prompted President
Kennedy to give a warning to Khrushchev on September 4. Then we
found some cruise missiles. These were coastal defense missiles, and we
also found guided missile patrol boats. On September 13, President
Kennedy gave his second warning to Khrushchev that the "gravest of
issues" would arise if they put in surface-to-surface missiles.

He was continually being reassured by the Russians that nothing
would be done in that way. So we had a watch on Cuba. We had a
report from a covert agent that there was an area in Cuba in which
Cubans were being moved out and Russians were being moved in,
and we decided to take a look. A U-2 mission was flown on October
14. It was processed October 15, and we discovered two medium-
range ballistic missile sites in Cuba.

When President Kennedy was briefed he asked that the whole island
be covered. A number of U-2 missions were flown, and in addition to

the two medium-range ballistic missiles sites, we found four additional ones in various states of construction, and three intermediate- range ballistic missile sites in the initial stage of construction.

The president ran his options, that is, his advisors on the executive committee of the National Security Council ran options from doing nothing to invading Cuba. The president chose a blockade.

On October 22 he informed the nation that there were offensive missiles in Cuba. Then he instituted low-altitude reconnaissance. These planes flew at about 500 miles-an-hour from 250 to 1,000 feet and brought back spectacular photographs on which we could identify every piece of military equipment.

This prompted the decision by the president to bring the matter to the United Nations. We prepared all the materials, and on the afternoon of October 25 Soviet Ambassador Zorin denied there were missiles in Cuba. The code word was "stick him," meaning bring out the aerial photography. On the night of October 25 there was an angry confrontation between UN Ambassador Adlai Stevenson and Zorin.

Zorin claimed he was not in an American courtroom and Stevenson said, "Very well, answer 'yes' or 'no.' Are there missiles in Cuba? I'm willing to wait 'til hell freezes over for an answer." When the answer wasn't forthcoming, the aerial photos were brought down on the floor of the United Nations.

Public opinion, both [in the] United States and the world, swung behind the United States, but the Soviets continued the construction of the missile sites. On October 27 we reported to the president that the six medium-range ballistic missile sites consisting of twenty-four launch pads were operational. That morning we received word one of our U-2s had been shot down over Cuba. They were also firing at the low-altitude airplanes.

They were digging trenches all over the island. The Soviets were attempting to camouflage the missile sites, and in addition the president received a letter from Khrushchev. The letter, according to Maxwell Taylor and others, was a troubled one. At the time they didn't know whether Khrushchev had been replaced or had his position made less important as premier.

When the information was presented to the president that night by Arthur C. Lundahl, the director of the National Photographic Interpretation Center, and John McCone, the director of the CIA, the president decided it was time for action. All during this period there was the largest mobilization of U.S. troops since World War II. Troops from all over the U.S. were being moved to Florida.

The Eighty-Second Airborne and the 101st were ready for jumps into Cuba. The 101st was to jump at Mariel and Baracoa and secure the port of Mariel. The Eighty-Second was to jump further inland and secure the San Antonio de Los Baños and Jose Marti airfields. The marines were to come ashore on the beaches to the east of Havana, then there would be a pincer movement to isolate Havana. They were to race to the missile sites and cut the island in half.

Khrushchev knew that an invasion was imminent. On Saturday evening [the 27th], Bobby [Kennedy] delivered an ultimatum to Dobrynin [Soviet ambassador to the U.S.] that the missiles had to be removed or the United States was prepared to bomb and invade Cuba.

On Sunday morning, the 28th, Khrushchev, in the clear, over Radio Moscow, indicated that he would remove the missiles. This was very unusual because normally this type of traffic is carried through diplomatic channels.

The president was concerned that the Soviets [might] be lying again. Again, low-altitude reconnaissance planes roamed over the island, and the next day, too; then we began to see indications that the Soviets were going to remove the missiles.

The problem was to count the missiles and make sure all of them were sent back to the Soviet Union. There was very close reconnaissance, not only of the sites but also the roads leading to the ports. Also, [there was] heavy reconnaissance over the ports as missiles were loaded, and then the missiles were observed on deck as the ships left Cuba.

The last problem was the Russians had sent IL-28 Beagle jet bombers to Cuba. Negotiations began in earnest at the United Nations [among] Stevenson, John McCloy, and Soviet Deputy Foreign Minister Kuznetsov. The Soviets agreed to remove the bombers, and then Kennedy indicated the crisis was, in a sense, over.

Much has been made that we had, at that time, sixty Thor missiles in England—intermediate-range ballistic missiles—thirty Jupiter intermediate-range ballistic missiles in Italy, and fifteen in Turkey. Much has been made that there was a deal struck between Kennedy and Khrushchev, but no such deal was struck.

The reason the missiles were moved out of Turkey was the fact that Polaris submarines had taken up patrol in the Mediterranean. The agreement, verbal between the United States and Russia, was that

President Kennedy would not invade Cuba, provided the missiles were removed from Cuba under UN inspection.

The Russians indicated Castro was getting hard to handle so the UN inspection never took place. Since the UN inspection never took place, there's a big question: *Did the pledge not to invade Cuba still exist?*

The Cuban Missile Crisis came very close to a nuclear conflict. The military had gone from Defense Condition 3 to 2. At that time there were some 1,400 Strategic Air Command bombers, many loaded with nuclear weapons, flying what was known as the HR Control Line: flying north to the Arctic and then waiting for an indication either to proceed to bomb Russia or to come back.

In addition to the bombers, there were always about 125 intercontinental ballistic missiles on pads. There were also nine Polaris submarines at sea capable of firing 144 Polaris missiles at the Soviet Union. In the event of war, there were seventy Russian cities scheduled for destruction.

Now, it was not only the Russians that would be the ones suffering from a nuclear holocaust. I was quite concerned that if one missile was fired from Cuba, it would be the one that would land on Washington. Of course, I had my family here.

That's a quick wrap-up of the Cuban Missile Crisis as seen from the National Photographic Interpretation Center, where I prepared all of the notes for the briefing of the president. Also, I prepared the notes for the four foreign leaders that the president decided should be briefed: Prime Minister Diefenbaker of Canada, Konrad Adenauer of West Germany, Charles de Gaulle of France, and Harold Macmillan of England. They were briefed before the president's speech to the nation on October 22.

This [was Kennedy's] shining hour because he looked at everything very objectively. His favorite word during the crisis was "prudent." He had taken the first step—the blockade—and then would be tightening the screws. He always indicated he didn't want to paint Khrushchev into a corner. He always wanted to leave him an alley to get out. It was his diplomacy, because certainly the military were looking upon this as a challenge.

Maxwell Taylor told me, "The Soviets have invested millions of dollars transporting this equipment and men to Cuba, and you don't do that with the idea it will fail."

The military looked upon it as a threat and decided it had to be met with an equal threat. An equal threat was the possible bombardment of the Soviet Union. The night of the 27th I thought was very, very close. Too close for comfort. Khrushchev had forty-eight hours, and he only took twelve of the forty-eight to make up his mind to remove the missiles.

Did this result in Khrushchev's being ousted from power two years later?

Yes. The Soviet analysts indicated that this was his unraveling, and two years later he was removed. It was a typical Khrushchev move: bold, aggressive, and poorly planned.

The Russians dropped Castro on his head. Once they saw the U.S. threat, they did not, to the best of our knowledge, consult with him. And he was furious, and the Soviet ambassador to Cuba couldn't handle him. They sent their premier diplomat, Anastas Mikoyan, to Cuba. When he got there Castro was a raving maniac, and Mikoyan, a patient Armenian, said, "You let a good cow bellow for a while before you milk her." And that's what he did.

When he met with Castro, he drew him up short. Castro said that he'd fight alone, and Mikoyan said, "Well, there won't be any Russians. That's exactly what the Kennedy boys want. They would like nothing better than to see you hanging from the highest light pole in Havana."

That chilled Castro. Castro knew the full military might of the United States was out there at sea. He didn't dare make a foolish move that would bring on the complete destruction of the island.

Mikoyan's wife died during this period, and he didn't go back for the funeral.

We talked to several Russians. They indicated that he never forgave Castro because this was a wife he had a lot of love for. He had to send his son home to arrange for her burial, and never forgave Castro for that.

[General] LeMay had created a bomber force specifically . . . to defend the United States, and he was ready to use it. He always referred to Russia as the "Bear," and he saw that we had a tremendous advantage over the Soviet Union. We had a strategic advantage of seven to one. The Russians later admitted that it might have been as high as fourteen to one. [LeMay said] [that] if they wanted war, they had picked the wrong battlefield and the wrong time.

Adlai Stevenson [was the biggest dove]. Stevenson wanted to negotiate the issues. That prompted a remark by Bobby Kennedy to the effect that Stevenson wanted a Munich. In fact, he said loudly enough to hear, "You got to put some starch in the son-of-a-bitch's back or get somebody to replace him."

The Kennedys never did trust the New York faction [of] Adlai Stevenson, Eleanor Roosevelt, Governor Lehman, and Averell Harriman—the liberals of the Democratic Party. The Kennedys were also leery that Stevenson might try to run again, so they cast a jaundiced eye at this New York liberal wing of the party.

I want to point out that President Eisenhower, in his wisdom, saw the need for reconnaissance systems. During his administration the "Genetrix" reconnaissance balloons, the U-2, the SR-71, and satellite reconnaissance were created. Concomitant with that, there was an organization created called the National Photographic Interpretation Center.

I was on the founding cadre, and we developed the techniques to look at this material, and we did it for one reason and one reason alone—to protect the security of this nation.

As I look back, I feel good that we've done a pretty good job of doing just that. We did it under a lot of odds, but once there was a good idea, there were men like Dr. Edwin Land and "Kelly" Johnson, who designed the U-2 and the SR-71. There was also Arthur Lundahl, the director of the National Photographic Interpretation Center. Through our efforts we maintained the peace over the period. That's the biggest contribution of all.

Do you believe the Cuban Missile Crisis was a turning point in the twentieth century?

No doubt about it. We had talked about going to the "brink." There were statements, [threats of] "massive retaliations," and the Soviets were saying "We will bury you." We will do this and we will do that. We got to the point of launching nuclear weapons. We looked around and wondered what stupidity our national leaders had gotten us into.

It was the unsung heroes like yourself who helped get us through this period.

That's the love of country. I had flown in World War II. I had flown in sixty-six bombing missions. I'd put my life on the line again and again, and then I realized that we had to stop that kind of thing. War: we should do everything to prevent it, and we did.

CHAPTER 26

November 22, 1963

Gov. John Connally

America changed on November 22, 1963. Vietnam, civil disorder, loss of confidence in established institutions, and additional assassinations would follow, turning the country inside out and leading to a splintered society.

I spoke with John Connally shortly before his death.

Early in 1962, President Kennedy told me he wanted to come to Texas and hold five fundraising events. I disagreed with that pretty strongly. I thought it was bad. Basically told him through friends of Vice President Johnson that I thought if he came just for five fundraising events that it would be regarded as a money rape of Texas, since he had not been to Texas since his election.

So I frankly stalled for several months until we put together a program that encompassed some nonpolitical events, as well as the proposed fundraising dinner at Austin, Texas, the night of November 22.

Once the plans were settled and we agreed, I was enthusiastic about it. Had a large hand in arranging the whole thing. Had personally gotten on the phone to sell tickets to the dinner in Austin. So there was no reluctance on my part when we reached that point.

[There was a] problem between Johnson and [Ralph] Yarborough, not between Yarborough and me. The stories were rampant that Kennedy came to Texas to solve the problems within the party between Yarborough and Johnson or Yarborough and me. Well, he had Johnson and Yarborough in Washington. He didn't need to come down here to settle the differences between them.

[The] problem started between them when Price Daniel was elected governor. But it really flared when Kennedy and Johnson were elected to their respective offices, and Johnson got a commitment out of President Kennedy that he would get half of the patronage of Texas.

See, Johnson gave up a Senate seat and John Tower, a Republican, was elected. Well, that meant all the Democratic patronage under Kennedy would go to Yarborough. Johnson got Kennedy to agree to let him have half of it. This infuriated Yarborough because it was normally senatorial patronage, and that's what precipitated the feud. I was no part of it. I had nothing whatever to do with it.

[The crowds on November 22] were bigger and more enthusiastic than I thought they would be. I thought there would be some nasty signs or shouts from the audience along the parade route, something like that. But I was not in the least concerned about any serious attacks such as occurred.

Do you remember your last conversation with JFK? Were you discussing a poll in the Houston Chronicle *that was coming out the next day showing you running a little ahead of him in Texas?*

That wasn't the last conversation, but that was a conversation we had in the car. We had been in Houston. He had talked to the publisher of the *Chronicle*, who told him about the poll, about how he rated, and in the car, along the parade route, he asked me, "How do you rate in the poll?"

I said, "Well, I think I rate a little bit better than you do, Mr. President." That was the extent of it.

We were commenting about the crowds. We didn't talk a great deal. The last conversation was with Nellie [Governor Connally's wife]. As we turned off Main Street and reached the relative calm just before the turn over on Elm, Nellie turned to the president and said, "Now, Mr. President, you can't say Dallas doesn't love you."

And he said, "No, you really can't." That was the last conversation anybody had in the car.

But along a route like that you don't do an awful lot of talking, because your mind and your attention [are] always on the crowds along the way. You're paying attention to them. You're responding to them, and it's really quite difficult to carry on a conversation, and we didn't carry on a conversation of any substance.

Did you hear the first shot?

Yes, I did. I thought it was a rifle shot. I turned to look over my right shoulder because the sound came from behind me and above me, and I looked to see if I could see anything out of the ordinary. But I clearly thought it was a rifle shot. Then I turned left to look over my left shoulder because I didn't see anything when I turned to the right. And just as I straightened up I felt the impact of the bullet that hit me, which was the second bullet. Could not have been the first.

I heard the sound of the first bullet. That bullet had already passed us. The second bullet I never heard. I felt it. I never heard, or was conscious of the sound of it, and then the third shot, I saw the evidence quite clearly. I heard it impact the president's head, and then I saw the results of blood and brain tissue all over the interior of the car and all over our clothing.

How many shots do you believe were fired?

Only three.

You were quoted as saying, "My God, they're trying to kill us all." Is that correct?

Yes, I did.

I was on the jump seat in front of the president. Nellie was on the jump seat in front of Jackie Kennedy. After I was hit with the second shot, Nellie pulled me down, my head down in her lap, then put her head on top of mine so in the film you can hardly see either of us in those jump seats. I was seated on the jump seat leaning over into her lap.

There was quite a loud, sharp slap—like you slapped your hands together. I was conscious, I was looking forward. I was looking into the back of the front seat. The car was covered in a blue velour material, and immediately after that loud slap sound I saw brain tissue as big as the end of my finger and blood all over the interior of the car and all over our clothing. I knew no one could survive it.

I knew it had to be the president because Jackie Kennedy said, "My God, I've got his brains in my hand." So, obviously, it was a fatal shot. He was instantly killed.

The Secret Service agent in the front seat said to the driver, "My God, get the hell out of here." I was in and out of consciousness and really didn't become conscious again until we braked to a very sudden stop in front of the hospital. At that point, to when they put me on the stretcher, is the first time I really began to feel the pain of the shot.

Your wife Nellie was disturbed because they tried to climb over you to get to the president's body.

That's correct. She knew he was dead. The door to the back part of the car was opposite me, and his seat, the back seat, was behind me, so it was difficult. They ultimately lifted him over the side of the car. Didn't even attempt to bring him out through the door. That's what was upsetting her, because she felt I was sitting there for an interminable period and no one was doing anything about it. I was still alive and she knew the president was dead.

As far as you're concerned, you were both hit from behind. You were shot once in the back.

Yes. Shot through the chest. It took out two ribs, I believe number five and number six ribs. I was holding my hat in front of me, and it just happened to be at a point where the bullet went through my right wrist and broke all the bones in the wrist and then went into my left leg.

Did the bullet that went through Kennedy go through you?

That's what the Warren Commission thinks. Basically, [it is] what the House Investigating Committee thinks. They think probably the first shot missed. The second one went through him and then me. All I know is there were three shots. I never saw him. I don't know whether he was hit with the first or the second bullet through his neck. I do know that he was hit with the third bullet, and that's all I can be sure of.

Do you believe the Warren Commission's Report?

Basically, yes.

Do you think there was any conspiracy?

No, I do not. I think anybody who alleges that is doing it for purely commercial purposes.

Kennedy had not been successful in getting his program through the Congress. He was having difficulty. Johnson though, in the aftermath of the assassination, passed not only the Kennedy program, but much more as well. So if Kennedy had lived, he would have had difficulty continually with Congress in the furtherance of his legislative program. He would have had a tough race, in my opinion, in 1964. I think it would have been a much closer race than it turned out to be.

This country began to change during his time. If you'll think back, a great many things began to take place. There was a revolution of youth in the country. It was all attributed to Vietnam, and I don't believe that. I think part of it was, but it went far beyond that. There was a revolution against religion, particularly among young people. They cast aside all tenets of faith. The graffiti on the walls of the country. "Is God dead?"

There was a reaction against any parental guidance. Young people were casting off all anchors of the school, the church, the family. The age of permissiveness began. The days of marijuana started. The rise of the women's liberation movement flourished. It really began to take off, and we're still in the throes of that.

There was a pervasive change that began in the 1960s. How much of it was directly attributable to Kennedy, I don't know. I think some of it clearly was. He was a symbol to the young people. He was a symbol of change. He succeeded Eisenhower, who represented the old establishment, and here came a bright young fellow. His wife characterized a change of fashion, of youth. So all of it was part of what began in the 1960s as a major change in the social structure of this country.

You believe his death accelerated that?

I think it did. I think it accelerated it in Johnson's programs. The Great Society also magnified it. The poverty program, the civil rights program. All the other things that Johnson passed were part of it— part of the sweeping change that took place in the country.

CHAPTER 27

The Vietnam War

George Herring

George Herring, one of America's foremost authorities on the Vietnam War and author of *America's Longest War,* says the turning point for us in Vietnam occurred in 1954. Ironically, Russia, as a result of Vietnam, believed communism was gaining momentum, which led them to war in Afghanistan and contributed to the demise of their system.

Our first involvement in Vietnam goes back as early as 1945 when the United States stands by and does nothing to discourage or prevent the French from an ill-fated and misguided effort to return to what had been French Indochina and re-establish their empire.

In a passive sort of way that's the first Vietnam decision. The first commitment comes in the spring of 1950 when the United States sends military and economic assistance to the French and to the puppet government the French have created in Vietnam who are fighting Ho Chi Minh's Viet Minh insurgents.

In the scheme of things it's a minor decision that only in retrospect takes on such enormous importance. It's not something that's debated, because they already have the money. They don't have to go to Congress. The money's in a fund set aside to use for China, which had just fallen in the summer of 1949, so it's a decision that passes without much notice. There's always going to be somebody somewhere who says this is a bad idea, and there were two or three people in the government who warned that it was a serious mistake to get entangled with French colonialism with the prospects of success pretty low, pretty dismal.

Dienbienphu is important militarily because the Viet Minh are able to defeat a major detachment of French forces, but it's a battle that takes on more symbolic significance than it should have. The battle lasts fifty-five days, attracts a lot of attention in the Western press, and ends literally on the day the Geneva Conference begins.

That conference was to discuss the fate of French Indochina. Therefore it has a huge impact on the deliberations in Geneva. It's interpreted rightly, of course, as a French defeat, but it's not a decisive enough Viet Minh victory [to enable them to] lay legitimate claim to all of Vietnam. As a result, you have an arbitrary division at Geneva [and] therefore the basis for a second Indochina war to begin only a few years later.

In the cities Viet Minh guerrillas are carrying out operations of one kind or the other, often quite small but on a regular basis. The French are mounting a series of large-scale operations in the countryside and in some remote areas, most of them designed to knock out Viet Minh main force units, most of which end up in disaster for the French. They go into the interior of the country in search of Viet Minh main forces, can't find them, turn around and head back for their bases, and the Viet Minh attack them en route, inflicting heavy losses.

There are various kinds of activities taking place regularly during this period, more than sporadic warfare.

Regarding the Geneva Agreement, the North wanted to have elections but the South refused.

Ngo Dinh Diem and South Vietnam in effect said "sit on it" and the United States backs him up, and the Soviet Union, China, and Britain don't challenge it in any way.

A big turning point.

Oh, obviously, in a lot of different ways. If the elections had been held—you could play these little counter-factual things—it's almost certain Ho would have won. What would have happened after that is hard to predict. There were enough people in the South who didn't want to be communists and didn't want to be under the North Vietnamese so there would probably have been conflict, but it might also have been a conflict that was localized and not part of the larger Cold War.

I would argue in terms of turning points [that] the last really easy time for the United States to stay out would have been in 1954-55, when if we had done nothing events would have taken their course. We didn't have much invested in the area at that particular time. There wasn't much at stake, our prestige, blood, and treasure hadn't been invested, and that would have been a good time to do nothing.

There's a small advisor team of civilian and military people there between 1954 and '61. But the insurgency begins to pick up a lot of steam in '61, and Kennedy between 1961 and November '63 significantly expands the number of advisors from hundreds to more than 16,000, and these people begin to play roles that go beyond advising. They're actively involved in combat.

There are some fragments of evidence to suggest that [Kennedy] was in the process of making up his mind, or had made up his mind, that after he had been safely re-elected in 1964 he would take whatever steps were necessary to extricate the United States from what he had come to believe was a quagmire. I'm not absolutely convinced that this is what he planned to do, but some people certainly make that argument. It's based largely on the fact that Kennedy in 1961, while pressed by his advisors to send combat troops, adamantly refused to do so.

His escalation in Vietnam is limited. His enthusiasts argue that after the missile crisis he began to think in terms of some kind of accommodation with the Soviet Union and began to look for a way out of Vietnam because it began to look to him as though it was going to be a disaster.

Kennedy was very reluctant to do anything drastic until after he had been re-elected. South Vietnam goes to hell in a handbasket after Diem is overthrown and assassinated, and it's impossible to say what Kennedy would have done when faced with the deterioration that occurred in South Vietnam over the next year.

I think the situation when he died was sufficiently fluid that he thought he could hold the line for a year, get re-elected, and then with a mandate, or with four more years, find a way to pull the United States out without losing too much face. But there's no indication he was prepared [to do it]. Every step you take that gets you in deeper, makes it harder to get out.

So in that sense, 1954 is the real point of no return. The more people you've got there, the more money you've invested there, the more often you said how important Vietnam is, the harder it becomes to disengage.

The really intractable problem is South Vietnam itself. We're trying to create an independent country in an area that doesn't have much basis for nationhood. Early on there was the assumption we could help create this. Then there was the idea we could provide the margin of difference in terms of help and advice. Then ultimately nothing we do really fills the vacuum. We're able to hold the line between '65 and '73 simply by the sheer force of our numbers and the size of our presence.

We come in in '65 with South Vietnam on the verge of collapse. We leave militarily in March '73, and exactly two years later it collapses. There isn't a solid foundation in the South for what we're trying to do, and we underestimate our enemy, a fundamental mistake in war, and never quite come to terms with the fact that these people are absolutely and unequivocally committed to unify the country and drive out foreign influence.

The changes in public opinion begin in late summer and early fall of 1967. And then Tet in '68 increases [discontent], and there's a growing sense that we either can't win or we won't win, and people holding both of those points of view reached the conclusion that we need to begin to find a way to try to get out of there.

I have a lecture I call "A War That Never Seems To Go Away." It's not talked about much, it's not visible and out in the open, but it still influences the way we think. That was confirmed by the commentary in the media on the twenty-fifth anniversary [of Vietnam]. Newspapers had whole pull-out sections and a lot of attention devoted to it.

The war in Kosovo had Vietnam hovered all over it. Anytime the use of American forces comes up, the memories and lessons of Vietnam are very much a part of it. The [John] McCain [presidential] campaign had a whole lot to do with Vietnam. Vietnam is what made McCain something other than an ordinary senator from Arizona.

The passion . . . a lot of the emotions have subsided. Some of the wounds have healed, although if you get in a group of Vietnam generation people and start talking about it, you can still touch some nerves and feel emotions very quickly.

Vietnam may have more effect elsewhere than it does on us. It's one of the things that ironically contributes to the demise of the Soviet Union. The Soviet Union read the tea leaves from Vietnam as a sign that their system was on the march and they were invincible. They got a bit of hubris and that led them into adventures in Afghanistan that turned out to be disastrous for them and played a significant role in their demise.

It's amazing. As much psychological and emotional effect [as] it had on the United States, I don't see its political effect being that great.

CHAPTER 28

Vince Lombardi

David Maraniss

Author David Maraniss believes the age of innocence ended after the Green Bay Packers won the 1962 National Football League championship. The Kennedy assassination, Vietnam, Watergate—a plethora of problems changed the country's dynamic forever. This Pulitzer Prize-winner is the author of *When Pride Still Mattered* and *First in His Class*.

Bill Clinton would not have played for Vince Lombardi.

There's a sense in American society today that it doesn't matter whether you do something good, bad, or stupid, as long as you become a celebrity. Vince Lombardi, while a man of strengths and weaknesses, represented something else entirely; that you achieve through hard work, diligence, teamwork, perseverance, and integrity.

His famous line was "God, family, and the Green Bay Packers." But it didn't work out that way; the Packers were tied for first; family was third, maybe trailing a little bit behind golf in some cases. He was so driven to win he neglected some other parts of his life. He went to mass every day of his life, and prayed for an understanding of the dilemma he faced, that he couldn't give his family as much time and attention as he felt he should.

His son and daughter struggled with being the son and daughter of a famous man. At times the son had somewhat of a love-hate relationship with Lombardi, but there was never a sense that he didn't love them and care about them. He had no personal scandals attached to him whatsoever. He lived a very straightforward and honest life.

He was the right man, in the right place, at the right time, and created this incredible synergy. I'm not sure that Lombardi, as great a

coach as he was, could have created the same mythological propor-
tions had he been in New York City. There was something about this
incandescent team, the smallest franchise in American sports, that
lent in part to its grace.

There was something about Lombardi that elevated the Packers
above the level of another winning team. It was the way he won, the
way he carried himself, and what he talked about. Also, the fact he
came along when the National Football League and television were
emerging together. There's a quote in my book from Steve Sobol,
who was part of NFL Films, saying with television and football we
were looking for a patron saint, and we found him in Lombardi.

After the Packers won the 1962 NFL championship, they were flying
back from New York to Green Bay, and it struck me as I reconstructed
that scene from interviewing everyone involved that it was the end of
innocence. Within a year Kennedy would be dead, Hornung would be
suspended, and the country's dynamic would change forever.

There are forces beyond any individual—cultural and sociological
forces—that change whole countries and the world, so I do not
attribute it all to Kennedy. I use his assassination as a marker. It definitely was a turning point. It brought in the era of Vietnam, then
Watergate, and I always thought of it as the beginning of the sixties.

His wife, Marie, said he died at the right time.

I leave that an open question in the book. It's true with the larger
culture, but particularly the sports culture was beginning to change,
and it would have been very hard for Lombardi. On the other hand,
Lombardi was a great coach who would have succeeded in any era,
with any group of athletes.

He was a man who knew how to adjust without sacrificing any of
his integrity. What he looked for above all else was an athlete who
had the will to keep going and to win, so that Paul Hornung, who had
a lot of attributes the opposite of Lombardi's, nonetheless was his
favorite player. As long as they were winners and gave everything they
had on the football field and were leaders, Lombardi would find ways
to work with them, and they would find ways to sacrifice some of their
flamboyance to play for him.

[Bill] Clinton and Lombardi are opposites in many respects. What
they both have is incredible perseverance and a will to win. But that's

about all that holds them together. Lombardi's whole life was shaped by the values of family, and Clinton grew up really without much of a family to shape his values. Certainly had no father figure in his life.

The man Clinton believes was his biological father was killed in a car crash before he was born. It's unclear based on the documents whether even that is so. I'm not saying one way or the other. But in any case, he never had a father figure and who knows how important that is in shaping someone's values. In essence, Clinton grew up in an atmosphere where he could essentially say, or do, what he wanted and get away with it, and he learned how to do that on a large scale.

In very different ways Clinton and Lombardi had the same capacity to motivate people. A difference might be that Clinton has an extraordinary ability to size people up when meeting them, determine what they want to hear, how he can move them by adapting to them. Lombardi was a shrewd psychological judge of people, essentially had his own standards, and figured out how to motivate people within his own sense of what was right and to win.

Clinton's potential was far greater than his performance, largely because of his flaws. Politics is different from football, so it's not totally fair to compare the two and how someone succeeds in each. But Lombardi's flaws were of a much different magnitude than Clinton's; [Lombardi had a] single-mindedness to the point of obsession.

There were times when he was unable to enjoy his life because he was caught in what he called the "addiction of success." His addiction was to perfection, as much as to success, and getting the best out of other people. It had a largely enormous beneficial effect on everyone around him even though he suffered because of it.

Lombardi's wife loved him to the end deeply, and his son, who carried the glory and the burden of his name, Vince Lombardi, eventually came to appreciate his father and now gives motivational speeches based on his dad's life and philosophy. It took a lot of understanding from Vince, the son, to realize he had a father who burnt so brightly that it was hard for any of his nuclear family to get near him.

The central love of his life was his career and football, so it made it harder for him to give the time to his family. He was so burnt out from coaching that it was easier for him to just go play golf and forget himself.

CHAPTER 29

Lombardi and the Packers

Willie Davis

Vince Lombardi's approach of making every position open, to be filled by players with the most talent, best attitude, and greatest desire, finally made the National Football League an equal opportunity employer. Willie Davis was the defensive left end for Lombardi's great teams. A hall of famer and successful businessman, Willie Davis is a winner.

I played four years of college football at Grambling State University. I was the second one to come out of Grambling and go into pro football, Tank Younger being the first. I think well over 200 players from Grambling have since played pro football.

I was drafted in 1956 by the Cleveland Browns and went to training camp. I had had two military deferments while in college, then was contacted two weeks after being in camp and told I was going to be drafted into the service. I left training camp and served eighteen months in the military, came back, and played in '58 and '59, then was traded to Green Bay in 1960.

Green Bay had been described as the Siberia of the National Football League. Paul Brown made a point if you did not play well that they could always send you to Green Bay. When it happened my first thought was, *Gee, I failed in Cleveland.* At that point I didn't realize that a trade was part of the business and sometimes it didn't reflect on the job you were doing.

Lombardi's greatest success was the simple, basic approach he took to the game. I remember teams like San Francisco and Dallas had all the motion and various formations. His attitude was, we're not a fancy team. We can't do all those things, we're not going to fool anybody. We're going to win because we're going to line up and go at the other team. We're going to win because we're going to overcome the strengths of our opponent.

When I was traded, my first thought was that I might go to Canada, where they had showed a lot of interest in me out of college. The first conversation I had with Lombardi he was certain and definite about the Green Bay Packers being a team of the future. Winning was not going to be an option, it was going to be reality. We were going to win, and we were going to win, and we were going to win.

The sixties saw the National Football League begin to change. When I first came into the league, there was an undercurrent, if not a proven fact, that black players in particular were put in the same position so one would beat the other out, therefore limiting the number of African-Americans on each team. You saw it many times, but Paul Brown started to change that.

At Green Bay, Lombardi had you win your job based on talent, attitude, and desire to play. There was no quota, no unspoken number of how many African-Americans, how many of anything there was going to be. Those who played for the Green Bay Packers were the players who performed best in practice and in the game.

This was a turning point because as we began to win, as we added more African-American players and we continued to win, there was this sense [around the league] of, wow, if we're going to win, maybe we need to take the same approach. Vince created this whole notion of getting beyond the petty things and stereotypes. There's no question in my mind that Green Bay had suffered from this in the past.

There is no question he opened the gate. In the midst of our success we were starting seven, eight, nine African-Americans on defense. If we had not won, it would not have had much impact. But we did, and he made Green Bay the envy of the league. He created the blueprint, the relationship with the players, the character of the team, the love, the togetherness at Green Bay. I think every coach, in every organization, went a little bit in that direction. Not saying they all emulated Lombardi, but they were aware of what Lombardi was doing at Green Bay.

The one ingredient at Green Bay that sustained us over our winning period was pride. Lombardi used to talk about four things. Dedication, that untiring effort day after day, time after time. Discipline, the personal discipline of doing the right thing.

Commitment, not just a commitment, but a personal commitment. And pride in performance. At the end of the day if you're dedicated, disciplined, and committed, and you stay focused and do it time and time again, his premise was this builds an environment that produces success and pride.

And it worked at Green Bay. All at once we were these little guys from Wisconsin, willing to pay the price, Willie was willing to do whatever was necessary, especially Sunday at one o'clock. We were going to show a lot of people that we might have been the smallest city in the NFL, but we were going to put on the best performance. It was always a matter of pride with us.

When I walk into the dressing room today in Green Bay, I look at some of the players and have the sense they're happy to be there. But you have the feeling they have no idea what preceded them. When I began at Green Bay there were three African-Americans on the team, and you were concerned about everything from a place to live to fitting in the community. We used to walk down the street and invariably you caught people looking at you, thinking not only were you a Green Bay Packer but you were an African-American Green Bay Packer. Today, people don't think twice about it.

The heart of the team stayed together for seven years, at least a dozen of us. I cannot tell you how many times I run into people in airports and some guy will ask, "Aren't you Willie Davis?" And the next thing he's giving me the offensive and defensive lineup of the sixties Green Bay Packers. There's something about it that says, "This was special. This was an important time."

CHAPTER 30

I Am the Greatest

Robert Lipsyte

One of America's finest writers, Robert Lipsyte has covered sports for forty years. In addition to writing for the *New York Times,* he is an author and television producer.

What do you consider to be the turning point in American sports in the twentieth century?

This will sound odd, but it was a press conference on February 26, 1964, the morning after Cassius Clay beat Sonny Liston for the first time. Liston had quit in his corner at the seventh round. It seemed like an inconclusive fight at the time. [Muhammad] Ali—Cassius Clay as he was then known—was a 7-1 underdog. It was generally felt that Liston was going to beat him.

The next morning it was an entirely different Clay that we saw. He was very quiet, said he was going to be a gentleman from here on in. He was very humble after all the posturing, yelling, and noise-making. Only a few of us remained to continue talking to him, some badgering him about, "Are you a card-carrying member of the Black Muslims?" and what does that mean?

He said he didn't smoke, drink, or fornicate; why are you giving me such a hard time? He went on to make his famous "in the jungle, lions with lions, and tigers with tigers" [statement] his own racial separatist cant. Then he said, and I have always thought it was a declaration of athletic independence, "I don't have to be what you want me to be. I am free to be who I want."

185

As simple as that sounds, at the time it was profound and revolutionary coming from the brand new heavyweight champion of the world.

I think the heavyweight champion has always been the most traditional, the most reflective of values, a kind of sweet-tempered killer. Somebody who inside the ring gave us the greatest thrills, but outside was really a model of decorum. You think of Joe Louis, Gene Tunney, Jack Dempsey. Jack Johnson was an aberration, and that's why he was driven out. But here was the modern heavyweight champion of the world announcing his independence.

Kennedy had been shot a few months before, and this was the era of the Beatles. There was enormous fear among parents that these four guys were going to turn sexual mores upside down and liberate the kids. It was the beginning of real ferment among black athletes. Not only was Vietnam starting, but the civil rights struggle was in full swing. In football major teams were torn apart because the black athletes were insisting on wearing mustaches or letting their hair grow. The crewcut coaches saw this as an absolute defiance of their authority.

There was a great fear that the most traditional aspect of American life, sports, led by the most traditional of our athletes, the heavyweight champion of the world, was going to be a continuation of this rock and roll revolution. And here was Muhammad Ali saying that I don't have to be what you want me to be. I'm free to be who I want. This led to his refusal to step forward and be drafted in 1967.

Muhammad Ali has been sanctified in American life. He's kind of the athletic Mother Theresa, but at that time he was seen as an enormously dangerous person. The government really went after him. I remember covering the trials, and there was great fear among the prosecutors and military people who did not understand Ali did not have a lot of clout in American life, but saw him as the heavyweight champion of the world, leading all the black men out of the armed forces. Then who would fight our wars?

It was a continuing escalation of his declaration of independence, and he was stripped of his heavyweight championship. His being stripped of his heavyweight championship was an enormous message to black athletes throughout the country; the message being you really can't buck the system. And that message absolutely worked.

In my mind, there is an absolute arc from Ali's declaration of independence, which led to his refusal to be drafted, his being stripped of the heavyweight championship, and today's incredibly self-indulgent me-athlete. Athletes saw what happened, how you could be struck down, and very quickly those athletes who were caught up in Ali's defiance of what was seen as racist American society were slapped down.

The best example, of course, being John Carlos and Tommy Smith after winning the gold and the bronze in the Olympics in 1968, in a very mild gesture for that time. Raising black-gloved fists on the victory stand, then—bang!—getting thrown off the team, thrown out of the Olympic Village in Mexico City. And neither of them, as iconic as their picture might have been, has ever really recovered in any sort of professional way.

Ali never recovered, either. He never got anywhere near the sponsorship and endorsement contracts that somebody of his enormous popularity and fame would have gotten. There's no question in his time he was even more of a world figure than Michael Jordan, yet never made the same money.

This was an enormous turning point in sports. It moved us away from the idea of sports as a crucible of morality, as character building, as a place for individual expression.

We began to realize that sports really operates as a reflection—this was always true, but we never understood it before—of society's needs, wants, and mores, and led us to where we are now, where sports is an extension of entertainment. That sports exists as live-action drama. That sports really is an extension of the rock and roll that everybody was afraid of when the Beatles arrived the same year Cassius Clay did.

I was at the fight and interviewed Ali and Liston beforehand. I remember losing my breath for a moment when the two men came together for the ring instructions, realizing for the first time how much bigger Ali was than Liston.

We're talking three inches taller, longer arm span, broader. Clay wasn't as thick through the chest but he was bigger. Liston was operating on a different moral plain. It was really to Liston's advantage to lose that fight. Had he beaten Clay, that would have been the end of it, and who was he going to fight next? There was nobody around. There was no reason for him to have fought Clay. Everybody thought it was a terrible mismatch.

There was a return bout clause. He and his people controlled the promotion. They would all make money. It makes more sense that he would not so much dump the fight, but think, *Who needs to win this fight? I'll get him next time, or at least get another payday out of it.*

Liston probably did throw his arm out, and I think he was getting hurt. If the fight had gone on, I think Clay would have beaten him. It's more complicated in the sense that there's no reason to suspect it wasn't a fix, but I have no reason to think it was. Clay was faster, he was younger, he was bigger. He couldn't take a punch, and he was chopping the hell out of Liston. So I don't know. It's the second fight that makes you wonder.

The one in Lewiston, Maine, in '65 . . . I was sitting behind Howard Cosell, and he had ABC do instant replay one hundred times, and maybe by the thirtieth or fortieth replay I saw the punch. I could be sold on the premise it was a short right. Remember, a short punch is much more powerful than a long one. All the power is early, and Liston was coming right into it, and it could have knocked him out. On the other hand, Liston seemed inordinately cheerful the next morning.

It was a turning point in how we thought about athletes, where sports was going to go for the rest of the century, where it is now. Sports has become an enormous entertainment industry, which it certainly wasn't in 1964.

In 1964 the National Basketball Association barely existed as a viable force. College football really held sway. How many teams were there in baseball? We were not that far away from the original rust belt thirteen . . . colonies. We hadn't made the leap into sports to where it is now. And Ali took us there.

CHAPTER 31

Sex, Drugs, and Rock and Roll

Paul Major

According to Paul Major, who was there, the San Francisco hippie scene lasted only a year. Flourishing in 1967, it quickly died because of commercial exploitation and the drug speed. Paul was a radical then, and was loaded much of the time. It took years, but he finally achieved sobriety.

My wife and I had two children, but in 1966, as a direct result of my drinking and using, I left my family and moved to San Francisco so I could get good drugs and good music.

I was enough of a loner that I fit in, looked like some radical or hippie or whatever at the time. I've always been a good chameleon, could fit in anywhere. You give me a bar with a group of airline pilots—I can be the best airline pilot for about five minutes you ever heard in your life. A quick study.

I left Newport Beach with twenty dollars in my pocket, drove up to Berkeley, and spent the next four months living between San Francisco and Berkeley in the back of my '54 Buick Roadmaster convertible. I don't know what my plan was. I guess I didn't have one. I found out there was a newspaper in Berkeley, *The Berkeley Barb,* and you could buy it for a nickle and sell it for a dime on the street.

I noticed at the top it said, "ten cents Berkeley, fifteen-cents elsewhere," and I immediately figured out San Francisco was "elsewhere." I went over there and was the first person to sell *The Berkeley Barb* out in Haight.

I was enterprising, still living in my car. After a while the publisher of the *Barb* asked me if I would be willing to do stores, so I started doing the newsstands and music stores and stuff like that. At that time the *Chronicle* and *Examiner* were both on strike, so there was no daily paper in San Francisco. I was also doing *The Daily Ramparts* and *Sunday Ramparts;* it was building.

The sports editor of that paper was Jan Werner, who later went on to found *Rolling Stone.* When the first issue of *Rolling Stone* came out, there was a distributor who backed out on him, and a friend of mine and I were called in, and he said, "Would you do this paper for us?"

So I watched the first issue of *Rolling Stone* come off the press at the end of '67, and I was drugging and drinking a lot, by the way. I had no responsibilities and a fair amount of money at this time.

I was working about six days a month, doing the *Barb,* the *L.A. Free Press,* and *The East Village Other.* Then the next week I'd do *Rolling Stone,* which then came out every other week. Sometimes my alcohol and drug use would get in the way of my being able to work six days a month. I'd have to pay somebody to run the route occasionally while I was messed up.

At that time there weren't that many hippies; [you] probably could put most of the hippie population in the Filmore Auditorium on a Saturday night. But we were very colorful, and there was all this stuff about free concerts. The music in San Francisco at that time . . . we had The Dead and The Airplane and a few others that made international reputations. So the music was the centerpiece. I don't know what drew all those people up there. God, I wish they hadn't come. By September '67, the so-called Summer of Love, all the original hippies had left. It had turned into a commercial enterprise by that time.

They closed the psychedelic shops, and all the people that were originally out there on Haight Street doing creative stuff were gone. It became a very commercial enterprise, and they didn't want any part of it. The whole original idea was everything was to be free.

It was like an enormous commune except you didn't have to contribute anything. It was nice if you did. They had stores; if you got tired of the clothes you were wearing, you took them in and gave them the clothes and you could pick others. No money changed hands. That lasted until the summer of '67 when it got all the publicity and everybody started pouring in.

At the beginning, the hippie style was the Beatles' Sergeant Pepper look, with the bell bottoms, Nehru jackets, the whole bit. Those that had any money did that stuff. They were the classy looking hippies.

Then there were the people we didn't know who they were or what they were doing.

At first the Haight welcomed all these people. They were colorful and lively and there was some money at that time. The Haight was one of the first successful, integrated, middle-class neighborhoods in the country, a lovely area, a lot of old Victorians.

Regarding drugs, at first it was almost entirely marijuana and psychedelics. LSD, primarily. Some meth, some sylic, but mostly LSD. LSD did not become illegal until the first day of 1967. Up until that time anything was legal if you knew where to look. The primary source in the San Francisco area at that time was Agustus Stanley Owsley III. It was said he made ten million off LSD before it became illegal.

I was always on alcohol; marijuana, sometimes. LSD—I'd done a couple of six, seven, eight LSD trips before I left Southern California to go up to San Francisco. Just was a party guy. No conscience, no nothing. The next thing to come along was speed, and a lot of us thought speed was what ruined the whole hippie movement.

It's a violent drug, causes people to do paranoid and violent things. LSD's pretty peaceful, and marijuana is just very peaceful. Those were not an issue. When speed, when the methamphetamines came in, it got a little wild. I can remember the first fights I ever saw there shocked the hell out of me. You'd get people that were paranoid and violent. The turning point away from peace was speed and commercialism, and people left.

The radical political people abused women. Whether it was the Black Panthers or whatever, women made the coffee and the food and spread their legs. That was their job in the movement. It was pretty nasty.

The original hippies were pretty philosophical people. They weren't calling themselves hippies at that time. I don't know what they called themselves, but it was a movement toward a free, open society. They found an area where there were fairly inexpensive rents in the Haight, and they set up basics—we'll supply your needs, everybody contributes, everybody gets taken care of.

It was a very peaceful, quiet, joyous situation. Then in the summer of '67 people started coming in from all over the country without a clue about what to do. Had no resources, no nothing, and there were people who took advantage of those kids. It was a terrible situation.

They were exploited sexually, emotionally, financially. The original people were not exploiters, but the ones that came later were. By the end of '67 most of the original people had gone to Marin or Oregon or someplace, and that's when the commune period actually began.

There were two different groups. The political people, the Berkeley side, they were the political radicals, the Abby Hoffmans. They may have dressed like the hippies, but there was an animosity between the hippies and the politicals. The politicals were saying, "Get up off your ass and do something," and the hippies were saying, "Lighten up and let it go." There was quite an animosity between the University of California political people and the hippies. The hippies thought they were uptight, too serious. They weren't having any fun.

The movement was the political side. There wasn't any hippie movement. It was all the politicals. They dressed like hippies, so the hippies got the political tag.

The hippies were trying to pretend the thing was still going on. The diggers, for instance, who fed everybody—they had a place I think on Page. They used to feed everybody in the panhandle in the park. In Berkeley they had another group that fed everybody. The Black Panthers originally were for school lunches and feeding the kids. And trying to keep themselves from getting killed by the cops.

The cops didn't have a clue. Secondly, these people were too weird, so for the most part there was an ongoing animosity between anybody that looked freaky and the establishment and the police.

It wasn't that anybody was a threat to anybody else, it was just they were different, and you know how the world deals with difference. By '71, when they bolted up everything, put iron bars on everything in the Haight, the only thing left was the music.

I don't really know if it accomplished anything. As I look back, it's difficult to say if anything lasting ever came out of it. Certainly the music. It changed the face of the music industry. A lot of creative people got into politics. Mostly they were political people to begin with. There was some fairly creative writing—not like the beatniks though. They didn't produce like the beatniks. We didn't have any Kenneth Patchens or Allen Ginsbergs.

It made people aware there was something besides white bread and vanilla. L.A. was nothing compared to San Francisco. The creativity and music was mostly San Francisco. There were a lot of very good people who wound up in L.A., but the really creative, different people were in San Francisco. There were the New York people, but a lot of them came out of the beatnik movement, like the Fugs.

It increased a lot of awareness. In spite of its coming and going quickly, there was more of an awareness of what was going on in the world. There was an idea that just maybe, if we stuck together, we could change things. It didn't turn out that way, but things have gradually changed. But then you wound up with Reagan as governor at the end of the sixties, and president in the eighties, so we didn't exactly go forward on that one.

I go back into the midwest and I forget things are a lot different there. You walk into a restaurant in Illinois, Indiana, there are people smoking all over the place. They are all white. Racism abounds. I don't know if it changed anything in the midwest, but it scared the hell out of people.

It took me a lot of years after that to clean up my act. I knew I wasn't going anywhere, but it didn't make any difference to me. I eventually got married in San Francisco and moved down to Monterey. That was in '71. I was still doing some stuff with *Rolling Stone*, so I was going up there once a week and had seen the difference in the Haight and how it had gone from a place of openess and joy to a place of paranoia and fear. There were literally iron gates on all the businesses there.

There wasn't any cocaine in the sixties. It was basically a non-existent drug. When it finally came out at the beginning of the seventies, it was considered a non-addictive, feel-good, party drug. I kept on with it until I had a period of sobriety from 1975 to '77. My marriage had ended. I'd read a book called *Games Alcoholics Play* by Claude Steinert. It stated if you could stop drinking—I was drinking then—make certain changes in your life, you could go back to being a social drinker. I stayed off for about sixteen months and didn't use drugs either during that time.

Started back to school working toward a degree in counseling and was doing very well, then started drinking again about March or April of '77. During that time I'd worked on a statewide political campaign with Tom Hayden when he ran for senator—my radical politics.

After that I went on to the first election campaign for Leon Panetta, one of my heroes. Not a radical. I was pretty involved, got on the Democratic Central Committee, did all kinds of stuff for him over a period of time when I was not drinking.

Then I started again and it all went, my schooling, everything.

I saw my mother in Florida in 1982, and stopped drinking for six weeks. No problem. I could stop any time I wanted to if there was a good enough reason. But I received a DUI coming back from that trip, driving from San Francisco down to Monterey. I was at a pretty low point then, and thought, *Boy, this is really getting bad. I don't want to do this anymore.*

I had a commitment that required I be sober, so I made up my mind, I'm not going to drink that day. But I started at noon in spite of myself, and I wound up at this event in and out of a blackout.

Blackouts were not uncommon at that time. I was only on alcohol. I quit smoking marijuana when it got so damn expensive and too strong, actually. We always looked for dope we could smoke and be gone 'til Tuesday. We finally got it and were gone 'til the week after Tuesday. I didn't particularly like it.

I'd had a therapist who had taken me to my first Alcoholics Anonymous meeting during that period of sobriety in 1975, '76, and '77, and I knew it wasn't for me. I didn't need anything like that. I was still doing very well at that time. She took me to another meeting in 1981 after I got a DUI. And once again I didn't see anything that appealed to me, left, and a year and a half later I got another DUI. That's the one I got after I'd stopped for six weeks.

I called my therapist again to take me to two meetings, and I started going pretty much on a daily basis beginning November 5, 1982. I had to go to court on my DUI and had to do a very short bit of jail time. Other than that jail time, these were the only meetings I missed for about two years.

I went every day, sometimes twice a day. I wasn't sure I never wanted to drink again, but I really liked the people. They were the kind of people I was always looking for when I was out drinking and never found, like I never found a bar like "Cheers." I never put money on the bar and nobody ever got drunk. Everybody knew your name. Wasn't that nice. And that's what I found in Alcoholics Anonymous.

I got very, very active. In two years I went to work at Beacon House, a recovery facility, and worked there for thirteen years. Retired about three years ago and got married, moved to Carmel Valley, and we bought a house. My life has really turned around and I owe it all to Alcoholics Anonymous, nothing else. I did not go to a program, drying-out place or anything else. But I did get very active in Alcoholics Anonymous.

It was absolutely the turning point in my life. I would have nothing materially, spiritually, emotionally, or anything else without involvement in Alcoholics Anonymous.

CHAPTER 32

The 1968 Democratic Convention

Mike Royko

Jerry Rubin, Abbie Hoffman, Tom Hayden, and a cast of hippies, yippies, and dispirited liberals arrived in Chicago in August 1968 to disrupt the Democratic Convention, and they succeeded. The late Mike Royko, one of America's leading journalists, was there and believed the accompanying tumult was the reason Hubert Humphrey was not elected president.

There was a lot of scare talk. Not just David Dellinger. It was Abbie Hoffman and Jerry Rubin coming up with all their bizarre threats. They were going to put LSD in Lake Michigan and make everyone high. A lot of silly stuff that some elements of the press played up and scared people.

But at the same time you had rational people saying, "Look, there isn't enough LSD in the world to put in Lake Michigan that would have an effect on the drinking water." They were talking about seducing the delegates, all kinds of nonsensical stuff. I didn't take any of that seriously.

My view of the convention, and what happened, has always been that if Daley had listened to Ramsey Clark, who was then attorney general, and his people, the whole nightmare could have been avoided. They knew the demonstrators, knew their tactics, knew their methods. They tried to persuade Daley this was not going to be chaos. Things could be handled in a sane way. But it was his town, his convention, and he was going to do it his way. He wasn't going to listen to them. It was his belligerent position that led to the thing getting out of hand.

A lot of people who weren't in Chicago didn't understand the geography. The convention that Daley was trying to prevent from being disrupted was at the International Amphitheater, out near the stockyards, forty-some hundred south. Lincoln Park, where they were, is 1600 North. We're talking a distance of about fifty-six city blocks, about eight miles.

So you had demonstrators congregating in a park that was bordered on one side by the Outer Drive and Lake Michigan, on the other side by part of the city's entertainment district, about eight miles from the convention hall. How in the hell was somebody in Lincoln Park going to disrupt something going on eight miles away?

The cops went in there busting heads [under] the justification they were violating the curfew. The park district rules are you gotta be outta there by 11 P.M. Well, that may be what the ordinance says, but it's never been followed in Chicago. I mean, Christ, people are in the parks sometimes all night. Nobody really pays attention to 11 P.M. People sleep in the parks. When I was a kid, hundreds of families used to go out to Humbolt Park, our neighborhood park. We didn't have air conditioning, and during the sweltering weather we'd sleep there. It was really unnecessary to go in there and start chasing them.

What they could have probably done, and I discussed this with Jerry Rubin years later, if the police had [announced] at 11 P.M., "You are violating the curfew. You have a half hour to get out of here or we'll move you out," and then waited until midnight, then said, "You are in violation of the law. We are ordering you to leave. You have one hour to clear the park." Then at 1 A.M. they do it again, and again at 2 A.M.

Well, by morning you have a bunch of people who are chilly, tired, exhausted. They've been up all night, afraid the cops are going to come in. There would have been this tired, haggard group of people who sat up all night in the park to accomplish nothing. That's all they would have had to do, keep them awake and scared. The whole thing was so mishandled.

You've gotta remember, we're talking 1968. You've got a bunch of cops, most of them from blue-collar families. Many of them grew up on the southwest side and the northwest side of Chicago with a view of life more 1940s and fifties than the view of life people in the parks had.

You had people with very middle-class values. They had already been exposed to rioting because of [Martin Luther] King's death. They were looking at guys with hair down to the middle of their backs. All the things they found offensive they had to deal with. You had the sexual revolution, the racial revolution, the drug revolution . . . all the things they believed were bad, they had been dealing with for a year or more.

There had been all kinds of things going on in Chicago, and they were at a boiling point. This was a very angry police department.

[The demonstrators] were looking for confrontation. There's no question about it. They wanted this stuff on television. Abbie wanted it, Jerry wanted it, the whole bunch wanted it. Tom Hayden, everybody.

[The police] could have held back. In Lincoln Park, where it all started, they could have held back there. This stuff about the terrible things they were throwing, hell, if somebody tosses something, that doesn't mean the entire police force is supposed to go berserk and start busting whatever head is available. They reached the point [where] reporters and delegates wound up in the hospital with busted heads. They were out of control.

[Daley said], "Well, nobody got killed." That was something he kept emphasizing. They preserved order and protected the city. I received about 4,000 pieces of mail, and it was about fifty-fifty for and against Daley. It didn't hurt him politically because Chicago and Illinois are essentially conservative areas. There was far more support for Daley and the cops here than for people like Abbie and Jerry. They represented danger and revolution and all sorts of things to the public.

Daley took the position there was some plot going on. He was going to be assassinated. He spun poor Walter Cronkite all over the ballpark when he was interviewed by him. Cronkite didn't know how to respond, Daley claiming they had evidence of a plot to assassinate him and others. It turned out to be a lot of bull, but it turned out to be bull long after it had gone out on the air. Cronkite was in no position to challenge him, to demand, "What evidence do you have? Show us the evidence of this plot."

Daley did a pretty good job of propagandizing, and he did so with the cooperation of some editors who developed a great concern for Chicago's image. The paper I worked on [*Daily News*] put out a special section that was pretty well handed to them, giving nothing but Daley's version of what happened—put together by his press secretary. Then we printed this crap—which was full of lies and distortions—as something that could be mailed by Chicagoans to people in other parts of the country. We had a staff rebellion over that.

I told the editor it was the most disgraceful thing that had ever happened since I'd been on the paper. But from Daley's standpoint it worked. Sure the delegates went away furious, saying they'd never come back to Chicago, blah, blah, blah, blah. But Daley didn't really care what some guy from California thought, or some guy from New Jersey. They didn't deliver votes for him.

My mail was not just from Chicago. It was from all over the country. The city's bungalow belts, the working-class areas, blue-collar areas, the suburbs, they were all for Daley. The younger people, anti-war people, they saw it differently.

The political loser was Hubert Humphrey, the Democratic candidate for president.

Sure it was Hubert Humphrey. With a sane convention, Humphrey would have been elected president. I think I wrote at the time that Daley exceeded his reputation as a kingmaker. Everybody always talked about how Daley won the White House for Jack Kennedy by stealing all those votes, which was nonsense. Votes were stolen not for Jack Kennedy. They were stolen for the Democratic candidate for state's attorney, because that was the priority. The precinct captains and city hall didn't [care] about Jack Kennedy. They wanted to get rid of Ben Adamowski, a Republican state's attorney, who was looking to get indictments against most of the top Democrats.

A partial recount showed that, yes, there was a great deal of vote fraud, but no, the vote fraud wasn't to benefit Jack Kennedy. The vote fraud was to benefit Dan Ward, the machine's candidate for state's attorney.

Daley had this reputation as being a kingmaker, but the only president he could really claim to have elected was Richard Nixon, because it was the Democratic Convention in '68 that persuaded a large segment of the population that the Democrats weren't even capable of holding a convention without it turning into a riot. Why should they elect one of them? Put one of them in the White House?

No question about it, Hubert Humphrey was the big loser in that convention, and it turned out to be a very close election. Had there been an orderly convention, his campaign would have been off and running, rather than staggering. And he would have won.

PART IV

Difficulty Is the Excuse History Never Accepts

(Edward R. Murrow)

CHAPTER 33

The Price for Freedom

Adm. James B. Stockdale

James Stockdale was shot down over North Vietnam and spent nearly eight years as a prisoner of war. As the senior officer, he led the prisoners' resistance to interrogation so they would not be exploited for propaganda purposes. He attempted to take his life to show the Vietnamese he would not give in to them. For his bravery he was awarded the Congressional Medal of Honor.

They [the Vietnamese] caught me with a note to my men with instructions on how to screw-up the Vietnamese, and I was going to be put in the ropes. They put me in a little shed to keep me on ice that night. First they placed leg irons on me, then came back and put squeeze irons on me which make it impossible to sleep because of the pain, made worse because my leg was broken.

This was just five days short of my fourth anniversary in prison. When the man came in to put that second pair of ropes on me he was sobbing. The next morning when they took me into the regular torture room, people had tears in their eyes. Pretty soon they started to play dirge music and I thought, *Ho Chi Minh just died.*

He had died, and one of the officers said, "We will bring you down tomorrow." I was coming up on four years in solitary confinement so, usually being alone, I relied on the tap code and other ways to get messages out to direct the whole prisoner operation. I was the senior officer.

About sixteen Americans were killed in those [torture] rooms, so it was a serious matter, and I figured the only way to let them know I meant business when I said "I'm not going to spill my guts" was to cut my wrists. I knew two things. That I was in the only prison cell in

Hanoi Prison—it was a torture room—that had plain, complete glass windows. Secondly, I was in the only room that had a light switch; the lights were always on in solitary. The officer put me in a chair and placed the traveling irons on, which allowed me to hobble over and sit on a toilet bucket. When they slammed the door and left the light on I said, "Now's the time."

There was somebody checking about every two hours. I heard the footsteps of the guard, and he looked through a peek hole. He didn't know I knew, but I'd spent more time in that room than he had. I said, "I've got about two hours before he'll be back."

I turned off the light, pulled the curtains back, and used the palm of my hand to break the little glass panes in the window and brought out a few spears about a foot long. Put the curtain back, turned on the light, hobbled back over, sat down on my chair, and started jabbing my wrists. The blood came out blue, and I thought, *That's not arterial blood, that's secondary blood.* I dug deeper and started getting dizzy, then fell over in a pool of blood.

About two hours later, this guy came in and saw what he had on his hands. I heard in the distance "eeyow, eeyow"—that was him, I suppose. I was groggy and pretty soon the room filled up with soldiers and people. They took this very seriously. You'd think it was no big deal, just let me die in that pool of blood, because they'd killed other people.

They had the doctor there and he was getting ready to sew me up, and this little old man, "the bug," we called him, the guy that had told me tomorrow they'd bring me down, said, "Why did you do it, Stoddale? Why did you do it?"

I said, "I got tired of living like a dog, and I'm not going to do it any more. I've been four years living like this."

We were shouting back and forth. The guards took my pajamas—the two guards who had worked on me that day—to get washed. They brought in a pair of shorts and arranged to have a cot brought in, laid me down on it, and bandaged up both wrists. A soldier sat on a stool at the foot of the bed with a rifle across his knees. Then they locked the door, and that was it for the night.

The next morning I'm groggy, and here comes the commissar himself, Major Bui. We'd had quite a history together. A history of tactics, trickery, but he was not a brute. He was kind of a sensitive man, and he would say to me, "You know, Stoddale, you and I are both college educated and we have sons the same age. But there is a wall between us, and we must see through that wall. It is the wall of the political system under which you work. You're a capitalist, I'm a communist, but we have to overcome that defect and between us we can stop this war." Well, of course that was bull, but he really felt that way.

After they sewed me up they put me back in that shed and wouldn't leave me—the doctor would keep track of me—until I could appear in a pair of pajamas and not reveal any bandages. I was under lock and key. About December they came and got me and weren't looking for trouble.

Two things had happened. One, torture as we had known it stopped two months previous when I cut my wrists. Secondly, the commissar had been dismissed. Life was never like that again. The next four years were a piece of cake by comparison. That's the turning point that I triggered.

CHAPTER 34

Why Communism Failed

Stephen Ambrose

Stephen Ambrose is one of America's premier historians and biographers.

I don't think Russia ever had a thought of attacking us. I know we never had any thought of attacking them. One of the costs of the Cold War was misperception by both sides. You always need to remind yourself that the leaders of the world, and the two superpowers especially, during the fifties and sixties, were men who had been burned in 1941. The Russian leaders had been burned by Barbarossa, the American leaders had been burned by Pearl Harbor.

There was a [feeling] . . . "We will never allow that to happen again. We'll never allow a nuclear Pearl Harbor to take place."

This fear of what the enemy might do was prudent, but also exaggerated by both sides. There were people who made half-ass suggestions—"Let's take them out now while we can"—and there may have been times when some mad scientists or generals in the Soviet Union said, "Maybe we can sneak one in on them." But people in power never thought about doing it.

Was there a plan to spend Russia into insolvency while building our nuclear arsenal?

Actually, Ike worried about it the other way around. He thought they could force us into insolvency with the stepped up arms race because they could keep taking it off the backs of their people by working them the way they did in World War II. Twelve hours a day, seven days a week for really nothing more than a little bit of shelter and a little food. You couldn't do that in the United States, and his fear was we would be the ones who would go bankrupt.

I don't accept the argument that we won the Cold War because we forced the communists into bankruptcy. The one thing they do well in that God-awful society is build arms. They make great tanks, pretty good airplanes, and good ICBM's. What they can't make are tractors and trucks, or grow crops, or get the crops to market.

When the Reagan people were saying, "We won the cold war because we spent them into bankruptcy," I always thought, and still do, that that's a strange argument for conservatives to make, because I would think a conservative would want to state the Soviet Union collapsed because communism is a rotten system. That's what I believe, and [it] was really reinforced by spending some time in the Soviet Union. It's just a rotten system, and that's why it collapsed in the end. We didn't spend Hungary into bankruptcy, or the Czechs. They're the ones that collapsed first.

Marx said they were going to create a new man. The first generation of socialism would be tough, but they would create a new man in this socialist system. You know what? The people that hate communism the most are precisely the ones born under it.

The old people of Russia [say], "In some ways it's better than the Czarist system. It's certainly better than the way things were during World War II. And it beats the hell out of being occupied by the Germans. We are fed and get a little bit of heat in the winter, so we'll stick with communism."

It's the young people who hate it. They're the ones who fled East Germany and forced the wall to come down. It's just a rotten system.

Ike was exactly right. He said, "We're in this for the long haul. It's going to take a long time, and we have to hold the line, contain them, and sooner or later it will implode from within."

And that is exactly what happened.

CHAPTER 35

The Fall of Communism

Adam Ulam

The late Adam Ulam was one of America's leading authorities on the Soviet Union. He was Gurney Professor of History and Political Science, and Director of the Russian Research Center at Harvard. He wrote numerous books on the Soviet Union, including *The Communists, A History of Soviet Russia, History of the Triumph of Communism in Russia,* and *Expansion and Coexistence.*

Was communist Russia ever strong enough militarily and economically to challenge the West?

No, there has never been a period when that looked likely. I think the most impressive period of Soviet industrial growth was their very quick recovery from the ravages of the war, which was really nothing short of miraculous. They lost 27,000,000 people in the war, about 14 percent of the total population. Half of the country was laid in ruins. Within ten years they were out-producing what they had been doing in '39-'40.

Stalin was smart enough to realize in the modern world it's industrial power that counts. The United States at the end of World War II produced more than half the industrial production of the whole world. The United States dwarfed not only Russia, but the whole world. The Russians had bled during the war. They demobilized fast because they needed men and women on the farms and in industry.

I know there were widespread fears in the West that the Russians could move to the English Channel within a matter of days, weeks. But it was ridiculous because the Soviet Union had been bled in the war. We had hardly been touched. Our enormous industrial power had been built up, never mind other Western nations. So those fears were hugely exaggerated even without the atom bomb.

You must remember that right after the war the communist parties of Italy and France were close to coming to power through legal means. Before 1948, each party gathered something like 30 percent of the votes. They were the most powerful parties legally in the West, and that was worrying us enormously. Their great popularity right after the war was very largely viewed to the prestige of the Soviet Union, which shed so much blood to win the war, and to the fact that during the war those parties acted as patriots.

After the Soviet Union was attacked, they became strongly anti-Fascist, led the resistance so their popularity was building between '45 and '48, but later started losing this popularity. They were ordered by Moscow to pause and sabotage the Marshall Plan, and of course that ran so much against the grain that their popularity largely declined. Still they remained strong, strong parties into the seventies.

After Stalin died in March 1953, the Russian leaders wished to change the system but did not know how to do it.

Yes, they realized that the power lapsed from a despot to an oligarchy of top dogs. They obviously didn't want another Stalin, of whom they lived in everyday terror. They were struggling for power among themselves and saw that without Stalin you cannot rule with Stalinist methods.

Strangely enough, the chief terrorist among them, Beria, the chief of police under Stalin, went furthest in trying to liberalize policies without of course jettisoning the position of the Communist Party. He wanted more liberal policies toward nationalities, better relations with the West. They realized they couldn't rule the old way.

They relaxed their rule over the satellite countries somewhat, and in '56 Khrushchev tried to reduce Stalin's stature from a deity to a party leader who did many wrong things. They wanted "the thaw"—that was the phrase for the relaxation from Stalin—letting millions of people free from concentration camps.

But Khrushchev said they didn't want the change "to become like a wave which would overflow the walls guarding our system." In other words, he was afraid what would happen might be what actually did happen in 1986-88 when Gorbachev started his reforms and they overflowed the borders of what was permissible in their eyes.

We didn't read [the signs] correctly. Right after the war we exaggerated the threat of Russia. We didn't exaggerate their intentions. They were always bent upon expansion. They had huge military power but our industrial power, nuclear bomb, and other things were such that it was very largely bluff on their part. Stalin felt the whole country had been bled during the war and he had to be ominous and threatening in order not to be pushed by us.

No communist leader, including Mr. Gorbachev, until he was compelled to do so, ever thought of loosening the monopoly power of the Communist Party over the country. And one should add that the Communist Party didn't mean that almost nineteen million members of the party shared in ruling the country. It meant that twenty to twenty-five people in the Politburo exercised effective rule.

They wanted to liberalize the system. They were in their own way humane men who saw the evil of the survival of certain features of Stalinism. They were not convinced Marxist-Leninists so much as people who wanted to hold onto power.

Gorbachev felt he could have his cake and eat it too. In other words liberalize the system, give it more dynamism, make it more humane, and yet have the Communist Party in the saddle as before and have the economy develop more vigorously. After a year or two things acquired a momentum of their own. People became horrified of the party, the party lost authority, and by 1988-89 it was clear the Communist Party was going to be replaced and that the country very likely would fall to pieces.

The administration in Washington believed until the last moment, August 1991, that somehow the country could be held together. In 1989 the Soviet Union let all its communist vassal regimes in Eastern Europe collapse. We realized that we were witnessing the decline of communism, but how much it would decline and completely fall to pieces the majority of the people, certainly the people in Washington, didn't realize until it happened at the end of 1991.

We shouldn't have been surprised at all, because what kept communism there in every case, without exception, was the fear of Soviet military intervention, as in Czechoslovakia in '68, in Hungary in '56. I used to tell my class years ago that at any point a Soviet leader should say, "Under no circumstances would we intervene, no matter what happens in Poland [or] Hungary," within twenty-four hours communist regimes would collapse. Well, I was a little bit premature.

It took a couple of months, but there it was. The Berlin Wall collapsed and the regime collapsed.

Communism needed the mentality of a state of siege. In other words, to contain its citizens, to persuade them that they were better off than people abroad, they had to feed their own people the idea the West is there. There may be temporary better relations with the United States, but the capitalists are always there. They're always scheming to overthrow our system.

Also, the whole foreign policy was sort of a public relations policy . . . they may be richer than we are. In this day of communications you couldn't pretend, as they did before Stalin's death, that they had a higher standard of living than the West. They said, "We are the wave of the future. Look what's happening in the underdeveloped world where countries choose our side." So they did need that mentality of a state of siege.

Did the arms race "break the back" of communism?

I think it played a very considerable role. As I mentioned before, they did a wonderful job in recovery from war in ten years. With the electronic revolution of the seventies they began to fall behind again, very largely because their resources, their best brains were concentrated on the defense industry. A huge portion of their GNP went to defense and certainly contributed to the decision of people like Gorbachev: we must change, liberalize in order to catch up with the West. But I don't think that was the main reason why communism collapsed.

The main reason was the complete collapse of ideology. The Sino-Soviet conflict showed there is no gain in having foreign countries become communist. On the contrary, Soviet security was endangered by having another country communist which became a threat to the security of the Soviet Union as they saw it. So, ideology declined.

For people at large, this ideology hadn't played much of a role anyway. They had not believed in it for a long time. They were apathetic about politics. Within the ruling class of Gorbachev's time, the younger people lost their nerve and felt they had to have reforms or the system could not continue as before.

I think what we call Marxism-Leninism is unlikely to rise, just as Hitlerism is unlikely to rise. There may be some other authoritarian version of socialism, but it's unlikely in the near future to prevail. But certain ideas, like planning the direction of economic life from the center, which are currently in great disfavor, may come again to occupy people. But Marxism and Leninism, as exemplified in the communist societies, including China of today, have been so sorely discredited that I don't think [they] will recur in our lifetime, or the next fifty years.

China is the remaining big bastion. Countries like North Korea and Cuba are just minor examples. In China, obviously, the rulers themselves decided that communism is not for them. They're trying to introduce capitalism. They have the southern zone of China where there is free trade, private property flourishing. In the second place, they've lost their proselytizing zeal.

So all those people, those veterans of the movement and their younger colleagues, hang on to power for power's sake, and not out of any conviction. I dare to think what will happen when that collapses because you'll have tremendous chaos again. Perhaps not as bad as what used to be the Soviet Union, because the vast majority of China's population is native Chinese. There are no major groups as in the Soviet Union. But the future of communism is very bleak everywhere.

Soviet leadership was, of course, very expansionist. But it was fairly rational in the realization that the world could not afford a major war.

Right now you have a situation where all those nuclear weapons are still interspersed throughout the old republics. Chances of some tactical weapons falling into the undesirable hands, the Iranians or Libyans, are not inconsiderable. Nobody knows what will happen in China when its turn comes to discard communism.

If we hadn't built up NATO, if we hadn't spent so much on our defense, they could have miscalculated and tried Afghanistan on a larger scale someplace and that might have led to war. Even though we were not in this dire danger of being overcome by the communists, I think our arming, our alliances served a good purpose and were not a waste of money.

I teach a course in Marxism, and I always point out Marx was a nineteenth century thinker whose thoughts were attuned to the early stage of the Industrial Revolution. So what he had to say was relevant and illustrative, if not always true, about the condition of the industrial world of the first seventy years of the nineteenth century.

Even by the end of the nineteenth century his doctrine was not so much wrong as it was irrelevant. Just like saying that scholasticism was wrong. The way people believed Christianity in the thirteenth and fourteenth centuries, scholasticism made a lot of sense. So, in that sense, Marx was not so wrong. Marx has become irrelevant.

CHAPTER 36

A Change in Direction

Michael Barone

Michael Barone is senior writer for *U.S. News and World Report* and author of *Our Country*. He is also a regular guest on numerous television news programs.

Three important turning points occurred in 1994. The first was the election of the Republican Congress in November and their essentially freezing spending for one fiscal year. That is a major reason why we have a balanced budget. If we hadn't elected a Republican Congress in '94, we would certainly not be looking at a balanced budget now.

The voters have a perception that this prosperity, to the extent it was created by elected officials at all, was a combination of Bill Clinton as president, and the Republicans as a majority in Congress. Clinton claimed credit for lower interest rates in the nineties, but in fact interest rates were rising between the introduction of the Clinton Health Care Plan in 1993 and the election in 1994.

They turned around on election day 1994, and interest rates went down and bond prices went up. This was a big and important change that obviously had a correlation.

We've seen a decade where American participation in the stock market has gone from about 20 percent toward 50 percent. The day Bill Clinton was elected the stock market was at approximately 3200. The day the Republican Congress was elected two years later it was at 3800. A 19 percent rise, nice, but not overwhelming. Between 1994 and today it has gone from 3800 to over 10000, coming close to tripling at some points, depending on where you measure the end point.

That is a huge increase in wealth for ordinary Americans, and almost all of it came when we had Clinton with a Republican Congress. Would the bond market have done as well with a Democratic Congress? I don't think so. Would the stock market have done as well with a Democratic Congress? My answer would be a confident *no*.

Clinton signed the Republican's Welfare Reform Act in August 1996, fourteen weeks before the election. Welfare dependency peaked in March 1994. Since then it has declined. The latest I saw was 49 percent, cut in half. Why did it start before the welfare bill was passed? Because the states were the ones that provided the real impetus for cutting the welfare rolls. And the states were experimenting even before the federal welfare bill was passed, which retrospectively approved the changes for which they had often had to get permission from the federal government. In some cases they just charged ahead.

Welfare reform of the kind we saw in the nineties goes back to Tommy Thompson when he took office as governor of Wisconsin in 1987 and since has cut the welfare rolls by 96 percent. Thompson's welfare bill went through many permutations and combinations. He changed—and we've seen it in state after state in the 1994-2000 period—the culture of the caregiving profession.

Previously welfare workers tended to measure success by how many people they could put on the rolls, how many dollars worth of benefits they could dispense. They did not see their job as providing jobs for people; rather, the contrary. Welfare workers now see their job as getting people jobs and getting them quickly.

Many see the requirements you're supposed to go through and walk out of the welfare office; they're not interested in welfare on those terms. Studies in *Public Interest* show that most former welfare people are doing well. That's a big change in America. Nobody predicted this, by the way, in the beginning of the 1990s.

Third change: crime. Crime, like welfare, approximately tripled between 1965 and 1975. Crime, again like welfare, is now declining and seems to have peaked in 1993. But for purposes of approximation we can say 1994 was a critical year, and I date it to January 1, 1994, when Rudolph Giuliani took office as mayor of New York.

Just as Thompson was the great generator and the strongest advocate of welfare reform and most creative, Giuliani was the most creative and strongest practitioner of controlling and reducing crime. He did a really miraculous job, and some of it just comes down to basics. He finally implemented the theory put into practice by the New York Transit Authority Police a couple of years before that: when you enforce rules against small offenses, you also begin enforcing rules against major offenses.

So everything from keeping the city clean, to preventing turnstile jumping in the subways, to tracking down people for arrest warrants that exist for minor crimes resulted in putting people behind bars who should be there.

The transit police, for example, found that a large percentage of turnstile jumpers were wanted for other crimes. They weren't just exuberant youth. These were criminals, and it made a tremendous difference here.

Giuliani's techniques were copied all over the country. Mayors began feeling pressure from their constituents saying, "Why can't you stop crime the way they're stopping crime in New York?" We stopped being a country where the psychology was: *We have a lot of people who have been discriminated against in the past, and they don't have much money. What can you expect? They'll commit crimes.*

We began to demand that people not commit crimes. And we're seeing a lot fewer people commit crimes, and I believe 1994 was the turnaround in that regard.

The election of the Republican Congress and consequent surge in the economy, the decline in welfare dependency, and decline in crime changed the life of Americans very much for the better. So 1994 was the turning point in this decade.

In all three cases—the surging economy, the decline in welfare dependency, and decline in crime—Clinton was an interested and occasionally helpful bystander. The real actors have been the people out there—not people in Washington. It's been people in the private economy, people who have changed the social work profession, provision of aid to people, people who enforce the laws against crime. Mayors, governors, investors, entrepreneurs, social workers, police officers—they have made the changes that have made America better. Clinton tried to figure out ways to get credit for it.

The reforms we're talking about suit the nature of society at the present time. In industrialized America, the solutions which tended to work were centralized, bureaucratic government, big government, the big units of society, big business and big labor working together. Those were the solutions that worked in industrial America. That got us out of the Depression, won World War II, and built a prosperous post-war America.

Post-industrial America in many ways more closely resembles the pre-industrial America that Alexis de Tocqueville described in *Democracy in America* in the 1830s than it does the industrial America in which we grew up. It is a more decentralized country, a more individualistic country than industrialized America, a country in which decentralized, market-oriented solutions work better than centralized, bureaucratic solutions.

As long as we continue to give leeway to the decentralized, market-oriented forces in this country, we can continue to make progress. Limit the control of centralized bureaucrats, subject them to the market force of competition, and you begin to get better results.

One of the problems with decentralized solutions is they're hard to see, particularly for people who are accustomed to looking at centralized political structures to provide solutions.

That's one of the reasons I emphasize specific individuals like Tommy Thompson on welfare and Mayor Rudolph Giuliani on crime. There are other people that none of us have ever heard of, like the head of the Welfare Department of Fond du Lac County, Wisconsin, which is on the leading edge of the Wisconsin reforms. Other governors and mayors—most of them Republicans, but many Democrats [as well]—have done outstanding and interesting work in these areas.

Richard M. Daley, the mayor of Chicago, is one of the players who is changing things for the better on a local basis—not looking for a national program, not coming to Washington begging for handouts—though he does that occasionally, but is actually changing institutions.

The city schools have been separate from the mayor's office for many years. Richard M. Daley took control of the schools by a state law passed by a Republican legislature and signed by a Republican governor in 1995. When given that power, Mayor Daley put in his own chief of staff as the CEO of the schools. The man doesn't have a Ph.D in education, although he did teach school early in his career. They have gone about raising what were abysmally low performance levels and have done it by a variety of means and shown creativity and energy.

The mayor has invested a lot of his own time, political capital, energy, and care on this, and it is achieving results. He didn't look to centralized Washington for solutions. He didn't look to the centralized dogmas of the education schools. Those are the forces that didn't work.

He figured out how to do it and he set goals, held people account-able, stopped financing the schools that were the worst, and removed people from them and held them up as examples of what was bad. He added more resources, encouragement, approval, and honor to those schools that are performing well.

CHAPTER 37

Do Not Depend on Your Friends

Joan Hoff

Educator and author of *Law, Gender and Injustice: A Legal History of U.S. Women,* Joan Hoff has been active in liberal causes since the sixties. She is dismayed by Bill Clinton, believing he set the women's movement back years, with a big assist from NOW for their abject surrender to political expediency.

I was appalled at the position NOW took regarding [Monica] Lewinsky and the general womanizing aspects of Clinton's personality. With respect to the welfare legislation, which they also supported, I was so disturbed I called a few friends like Robin Morgan and Gloria Steinem and told them I was going on CNN to comment on it and said, "I really don't know what to say. I can't understand it."

NOW has never been, even in its inception, a radical organization. In lieu of radicalism, Betty Friedan and others decided they'd better put together a group that was more moderate and more acceptable to the American people. It's always been a reformist kind of group. That's one reason you would see NOW perhaps siding with the Clinton administration on some pieces of legislation which really harm poor women, like the welfare legislation.

The NOW governing board, because of the return of prosperity, is made up of upper-middle-class women. Consequently, they are not as concerned about the condition of poor women or poor people in general as the organization once was.

In other words, prosperity breeds this more moderate, more selfish view on the part of groups which were once championing the greatest good for the greatest number. I don't think they are any longer.

NOW, with respect to Clinton's sexual behavior, and their support of him and of Hillary, who supports him, has set the women's movement back. We fought twenty-five years to get the "personal is political" to be a legitimate slogan and have meaning. With one swipe of the hand, NOW, with the support of Clinton and Hillary's support of her husband, write that off the political agenda. It's a meaningless slogan now with respect to the Democratic women who have steadfastly supported [it].

Initially, people laughed at it—what does that mean? The women's movement argued that your personal views are going to ultimately be reflected in your public actions. It was necessary for women and men to look at whether or not their private actions reflected their liberal political stance. And nine-tenths of the time, of course, they didn't.

The Civil Rights Movement, the Anti-War Movement were incredibly sexist and exploitative of women. That's one of the reasons you had women breaking away from those two groups and forming their own movement in the late 1960s, and it became this extremely important slogan for the entire movement.

By supporting Clinton's womanizing, and by denying that his private views of women and his use of women in a despicable fashion has nothing to do with what he has done in public, [they have] wiped out twenty-five years of work to establish that as a meaningful slogan.

Technically speaking, the women's movement was the only movement to survive the eighties. The movement survived better than the Civil Rights Movement did. That's been defunct for some time. But the women's movement survived the eighties only to be harmed and neutralized by Democrats. [It was done] by the very home base most women reformers had felt comfortable [with].

The turning point was the Clinton Administration . . . I can't say enough bad things about that piece of welfare legislation. It did in poor women. The figures show there's been a 60 percent increase in major cities in shelters housing women and children. And all these damned governors and mayors are saying, "Oh, look, our welfare rolls are down." They're not saying, "Look our shelter rolls are up."

Clinton moved the party to the right. He adopted Republican policies. The foreign policy analogy is Kosovo. We say we're going in there for humanitarian reasons and there aren't humanitarian results. It paralyzed the peaceniks. You don't know how to criticize something like that because the rhetoric is, "Oh, isn't this wonderful.

We're humanitarian," and then you have hundreds of thousands of people dislodged because of our humanitarian action and people killed on the ground because we won't send in ground troops.

The same thing happened with respect to welfare legislation. They reform it so it's harmful to more poor people. And this from the so-called more liberal of the two parties. The NOW board, after a big debate, signed on to that legislation. The Democrats have adopted the policies of the Republicans, leaving women and other reformers totally confounded with no place to go.

CHAPTER 38

Addiction

David

David has had a difficult life. But now his problems are coming to a head, and he is afraid he might lose his life.

I was born in 1944 and took my first drink around age six. Started sneaking into my mom and dad's liquor cabinet—didn't get drunk but just was curious, wanted to taste it. I started smoking cigarette butts out of the silent butler and then hiding them, putting them out in the binders of books. I would blow the smoke out my air conditioner; I learned to be sneaky early.

I had a lot of problems with rage when I was a kid. Both my mom and dad modeled perfection for me as an achievable goal, so I set myself up to reach for it. But no matter what I did, it was never enough. My mom was a rager, my dad passive, silent, and raged internally. He used nicotine, smoked a pipe, occasionally drank, and hid in his work. So my dad was gone behind work, my mom was gone behind alcohol.

I learned to rage with sarcasm, cynicism, and humor—sideways humor. I also raged overtly by yelling, screaming obscenities, primarily at my mother. My childhood, from the time I can remember to the time I left home and went to a military academy at the age of thirteen, was spent primarily being sneaky and raging. Coming back from a rage attack with my tail between my legs and learning that cycle of violence as a way to get love.

I learned I could be bad and then be sneaky and suck my feelings down with either alcohol or tobacco, then act badly and come back and have my dad be forgiving and my mom be judgmental, then ultimately forgiving because my dad said so. I had a twisted picture of relationships.

In 1962 I graduated from military school, and I went to college and fell madly in love with a girl. I behaved in compulsive, addictive, dependent ways with her—sexually, physically, emotionally, intellectually. As a consequence, I flunked out of school after my freshman year. I ended up with a 1.0 GPA [grade-point average], didn't do alcohol, didn't do drugs, but I transferred my compulsive, dependent, obsessive thinking onto sex.

When I flunked out I immediately went into the navy and the hospital corps. Whether that was subconscious or not, I was able to protect my supply. I was stationed at a small station hospital and worked in the pharmacy. I experimented with all kinds of drugs from amphetamines to hynotics to sleeping pills to pill drugs and became addicted to speed, to amphetamines.

They were not a controlled substance at that time. I had a can of a thousand dexamile in my room. That's fifteen milligrams of dexadrine or dextro-mephetamine sulphate and two and a half milligrams of amobarbitol.

It would be like a cocaine high, only the amobarbitol—which is a barbiturate—would kind of ease the coming out of the high. You'd be up for twelve hours grinding . . . your teeth, amped up, moving from one compulsive behavior to the next, not really thinking clearly. In some ways that is how I got through the navy until I went to Vietnam.

I went to Vietnam for the last year and a half of my four-year enlistment, and I didn't do anything. I was on a hospital ship. I figured I was being watched fairly closely, so I didn't smoke dope, didn't take pills. But when I went ashore on liberty every forty to sixty days, I got totally [wiped out] on alcohol. Used every opportunity when I went on liberty to get drunk and act stupid. The first time I'd really gotten into drugs was when I was in the navy, but I shut it off.

So it's the seventies now. I got out of the navy, went to college, continued to drink. A little junior college in Connecticut. Didn't graduate. I was married at the time and moved to California.

I was a veteran of probably seven junior colleges before I finally got a baccalaureate degree in nursing at the University of California at San Francisco, School of Nursing, in 1979. Got an associate in science degree the year before. I shined at UCSF, loved the school, but drank consistently. I worked as an ER [emergency room] nurse in a small hospital north of San Francisco. Smoked dope, and that's when I got into cocaine a bit.

It was scary to me, I didn't want to get involved in it, snorted it maybe ten times. Still, I was able to shore myself up by looking good on my job. This was 1980 to 1984. I was not satisfied with being a nurse, I wanted to go to medical school 'cause one of my greatest dreams was to become a physician. The delusion was I would be physician to the planet, I'd be physician to the world, and I wasn't sure I could do it.

I spent four years in Petaluma, went to Sonoma State University, and did prerequisites for medical school. At the same time I was smoking pot regularly. Not drinking very much, but I was binging. Once a month I'd get totally . . . drunk. But I was smoking stems, dirt weed, seeds, anything I could get my hands on. Very rarely would I get any pot that was of any value, and it affected my ability to get good grades in the prerequisites I was studying at Sonoma State.

Pot affects your short-term memory. It affected my ability to recall information, so when I took the medical college admission test, I blew it. In typical addictive form, doing well, looking good, and then on the other end doing something to sabotage the process—a cardinal feature of alcoholic addictive behavior. You either look bad all the time, or you look good and act bad, or you look good for a long time and then do something to sabotage it, do something to really mess it up.

That's what I've consistently done all of my life. I reach a point and then for whatever reason . . . some people say its just 'cause you're alcoholic. Some people say it's because of carried shame from your childhood. Some say it's because of what you brought on to the planet spiritually. I don't quite believe that.

But despite the cause, the behavior is consistent with what volumes of research show about addiction, and that is you start out very often experimenting and the process progresses to the point where it begins to affect your relationships and somebody will bony-finger you or point out to you they think you have a problem. Then you go underground, get sneaky.

I finished my prerequisites and I was finally accepted to medical school, finished the first year, and during that time I was raging. Wasn't drinking, wasn't using, I was raging. For example, screaming and yelling at anybody who made noise while I was trying to study. We lived in a house, my wife and I and my son. Other medical students lived in other houses around us, and they'd be jacking around at eleven o'clock at night, and I'd be under the gun trying to figure out how to do biochemistry problems or histology or something. Ultimately my wife took my son and moved out.

That was a turning point. It dropped me into the deepest pain I've ever felt and I did it sober. Finally, for the first time in years after not looking good, embarrassing my son, embarrassing my wife—my son was then four—I had to lay it down and say I needed help.

At that point I returned home and got into recovery, started seeing a therapist. I came through the back door into AA [Alcoholics Anonymous]. Saw a therapist who was very knowledgeable about addictions. She said to me, "Someone says you have a problem about your drinking. How are you going to look at that?"

I said, "Well, I suppose I could go to AA meetings, but I don't want to go to any smoking meetings, I am a smoker." 'Cause I didn't want to look bad. From the very beginning I've had this thing of needing to look good, but in order to recover I gotta lay that down. I've gotta just lay it down and be one of many, instead of being better than others.

Six months later I went to an organized program as a registered nurse. I was working in a treatment facility. Six months sober. I got the essence of treatment by not having to do treatment as a patient but as a clinician. It's the way someone who didn't want to be noticed would do it. Sneaky? That is very sneaky.

I divorced my wife. My child is with me. We shared custody at that time. Within two years, in 1985, I got back into another relationship with a woman who has two children and she's also recovering, and we began to recover together. We ultimately moved in together, blended our families.

In 1988 I stopped working in the treatment facility, and I had the bright idea we should talk to nurses about their co-dependency. Candace and I wrote a book called *I'm Dying to Take Care of You: Nurses and Co-dependents Breaking the Cycle*. We traveled around the country, traveled to Europe. We traveled to London doing lectures, seminars, group work, and really got off on that.

In 1991 Candace became ill with chronic fatigue immune deficiency disease. She stopped working and that meant I was the one who had to struggle to keep the business in place. It was clear the spiritual ingredients of our work together rested with Candace. I knew how to look good, she knew how to bring the essence of spirituality to our work. I was like an abalone on her rock and when she left I fell off and was floundering.

We are still married, doing very well. But back in 1994 I realized I needed more money to support her and the children so I went back to work in the insurance business. Health insurance—working for the government.

I maintained a private practice as an intervention therapist, intervention counselor, and that's something I've developed along with some clinicians at the recovery center. I had a private practice doing that and a public practice doing nursing insurance work. I was working fourteen hours a day, sucking down my feelings with nicotine, not participating much in recovery, not going to many meetings.

Not believing in a higher power, or a power greater than my addictions, or greater than Candace, or greater than my parents, or greater than the shame, or any of that sort of business . . . ultimately in 1998 I relapsed. I drank again, a totally miserable experience.

One of the things I'd heard as a clinician was that the disease is progressive. It gets worse over time, never better. That you can stop drinking for a long period of time, start again, and your body reacts as if you've been drinking all along because of the cellular memory. I don't know if it's true for everyone, but it's true for me.

Over that thirteen-year period from '85 to 1998, I'd been to men's alternatives to violence. I'd learned how to resolve the rage attacks I was having. I was in therapy with and without Candace, over many years, because we were driving a broken car and it needed a lot of tuning up. She had her issues, I had mine. Each of us had been married more than once, each had children from a former marriage. We were really like a size-eight hand in a size-seven glove. We were so enmeshed and when we started to do our individual work it felt like my guts were being ripped out.

One of the things I didn't know how to do was intimate relationships. I'd always been searching for a level of intimacy that addictions robbed me of—if I can end my sentence in a preposition. The intimacy, as a result of working with sponsors and being around other recovering men, isn't going to come from my penis. It's not going to come from smoking, from work, from anything that I can switch to with the speed of light whenever I think anybody is looking.

Chemical addictions aside, I have a lot of process addiction, sexual addiction, fantasy addiction where I can continue to do the same self-absorbing, self-seeking behavior to the point of harmful consequence, and the consequence for that behavior is my children will say to me, "I miss you. Where are you? Where have you been?"

The model of behavior I had for a father is that fathers are gone. They hang out and pay bills every night so as to avoid not having to talk to mom, who's drunk. Candace is not drunk, she's sitting there saying, "Where are you? Where have you been?"

And I'm saying, "Oh, I'm in here justifying my behavior. I'm doing Quicken." Or, "I'm paying the bills."

I have one daughter, thirty, married very happily, living in North Carolina. Both she and her husband are successful. No children. I have another son in college in Northern California, and I have another son who is an entrepreneur and has started his own business at the age of twenty, doing very well.

I'm told the only way I can have the obsession to drink and use removed is to humble myself before a power greater than my addictions or a power greater than my thinking, greater than myself. Because of my cynicism I give myself a lot of power in doubting the existence of any of that. I can go down a rosy path with that, but the bottom line is the cycle of self-destructive behavior comes back to bite me. I feel humiliated, I feel shame, and the shame is the motivator for me to get help and be a good little boy for a time. But then, deep inside, I don't trust that unless I do something different.

Unless I get it, unless I do something, I'm going to end up dead. I've been hurting as a result of the relapse, as a result of the self-deception, the lies to others, minimization, denials, illusions—those kinds of things—and it's really a struggle for me to get past my head, to get past my thinking.

Right now I'm doing a meeting or two a day. It is definitely day-to-day. I'm working with my sponsor and he's putting fire in my brain. He's burning up all those old ideas. Day at a time. I've got the path down, I taught it for so many years. Right now I have to get humble enough to say, "I'm hurting and I don't want to do this any more. Don't want to lose my marriage. Don't want to lose my children. Don't want to lose my life."

I think I could lose my life in a car accident being drunk, driving a car, going over a cliff, hitting a pole, hitting a tree, slipping into a coma, having a stroke. That's a form of suicide. It's risk-taking behavior.

CHAPTER 39

The American Dream

Don Boodel

Many times the difference between success and failure is self-discipline, continuing to work at something no matter the pain, trouble, and heartache. How many potential successes have withdrawn from the battlefield because they could not stick it out?

For Don Boodel, the acid test was twelve cents.

In the fall of 1958 I was attending the University of Illinois—nineteen at the time, studying physical education. I got a call from my father saying he'd like to talk to me about a business proposition, so the next time we got together we discussed the idea of buying a McDonald's franchise.

My father was a brassiere salesman, covering eleven states in the midwest. Traveling, he began seeing McDonald's popping up in the mid-fifties [and] would stop occasionally, have a sandwich, and started talking to some of the owner-operators. [He] became fascinated by the business. But he was concerned because it was a new business, and a lot of them were struggling. He knew he couldn't do that and sell brassieres at the same time, so he approached me with the idea that I join him in this venture along with my brother-in-law.

We didn't know where we would be located. We knew it wasn't going to be in the Chicago area, where I grew up. We discussed rather than becoming a manager for him, I start in training. We agreed the difference between how much money I would be making normally and the eighty-five cents an hour I'd be making as a trainee would be my investment in the business.

So in 1959 I left school and went to work for the McDonald's in Evanston, Illinois, training at eighty-five cents an hour. In those days it was a red-and-white tile building with arches. There was no seating; people would come in, buy their food, and eat in their cars. That sounds strange today but that's the way it was then. It was just hamburgers, cheeseburgers, french fries, milk shakes, and drinks. That was the entire menu.

By 1960 the owner-operators I was working for decided to open a McDonald's in Youngstown, Ohio, and wanted to know if I'd go down there for them. In those days it was not unusual to have multiple owners; three, four, five people getting together, pooling their money, assigning one as the working owner-operator, and opening their stores in that fashion.

This particular operation had six owner-operators but they wanted to train a brother who was a salesman in California to operate this McDonald's. I went down there with him—the spring of 1960—and opened this McDonald's in Youngstown. I'd been given a raise from eighty-five cents to $1.25 an hour, and I worked sixty straight days until I felt comfortable that the owner-operator, this gentleman in his sixties, would be capable of running it for the other investors.

At that time there were about 200 McDonald's operating throughout the United States, and the first and second month I was there we were number eight in sales in the United States.

When I got back to Chicago, the guys decided I'd done such a good job they gave me a $50 bonus, which amounted to less than a dollar a day for the sixty straight days that I worked.

By early 1961, McDonald's called us in and identified a couple of locations where we could go. We wanted to be in a big city, be able to expand some, and when Cleveland came up, we took it.

My dad stayed in Chicago and continued selling brassieres. I got my work ethic from him. He traveled those eleven states mostly by car and left in the wee hours of the morning on Monday and would come back late on Friday night. That doesn't sound like much of a life but that's the way people did it in those days. Nowadays it's all by phone and fax, but in those days if you were going to be a salesperson you had to make calls personally on all your clients.

We opened in Cleveland on September 20, 1961. Did $223.73 for the day, serving people fifteen-cent hamburgers. The rule of thumb was to hit $1,000 a day. As the fall progressed, we did a little better. This was the first and only McDonald's on the west side of Cleveland. I worked seven days per week, fifteen hours per day, opening and closing the restaurant. That routine lasted eleven months. At twenty-two I was the youngest owner-operator in the country.

We began to grow a bit, more stores came to the west side of Cleveland, and we began talking about mutual advertising, which had never been done by any group of McDonald's operators before.

By December I finally had a very good day with $1,000 in sales. But things were not turning [out] as we wanted them. I was barely paying myself, and my father was not drawing any money. Things looked bleak in January, with very snowy weather, and with it very little sales.

I specifically remember one day in February when we were hit by a tremendous snowstorm. I got up early because I was worried about what might happen. I got there at 7 A.M., and by 8 A.M. I received phone calls from the crew saying they couldn't make it in—both of them. At about 10:30 A.M. the snowplow guy comes in and does his job, then comes up to the window and wants a hot chocolate. I sold him the hot chocolate for twelve cents. He said, "You're charging me for it?" I said, "Well, you just charged me $35 to plow the lot."

I went through the day, closed the store that night, and cleaned up, took the cash register drawer to the back, put it on the desk, counted it out. I took out a bank deposit slip, made it out for twelve cents, took the dime and two pennies, put them in a bank bag, took it to the bank, and made a night deposit.

I talked with my father later that week and explained how things were going. I'll never forget breaking down and sobbing. We'd just had this twelve-cent day and I thought, *Everything this fifty-three-year-old man has worked for all his life is going to end up for nothing.* But I hung on, and by the middle of March things really started to pay off. All the hard work, focus, perseverance, enthusiasm, self-discipline, dedication, and long, long hours started to pay off. Sales grew, volume grew.

The operators in Cleveland at the time, there were six of us, decided to pool some of our money, putting 3 percent of our sales in the first McDonald's advertising cooperative. Until that time the only advertising materials we had were little mats we got from McDonald's Corporation that you'd put in your local newspaper. One for a cheeseburger, one for a milkshake, one for fries. We decided to go on kids' TV. Absolutely unheard of at the time.

We advertised a hamburger, french fries, and a milk shake, and we called it "The All-American Meal," forty-five cents and two cents tax. Forty-seven cents for a complete meal. Things began to happen. In

October 1962, our first comparable sales month, I led the country with a 95 percent sales increase.

At that time I called my parents in Chicago and told them to come to Cleveland. They moved there and my father would come in every day and be my "go-for." He was in semi-retirement from that point on. He never cooked a burger. He never fried fries. He never waited on a customer.

One thing led to another. I licensed a couple of more stores and by the time the early seventies rolled around, I decided Cleveland was not the place I wanted to end up. I spoke with McDonald's and they said, "Well, we could use somebody with your expertise in Denver. We have a special need out there." I flew out to Denver, took a look, realized my family could be happy there, I could be happy there, and that's where I am now.

I just celebrated my fortieth year with McDonald's, and over that period of time I've opened and run eleven McDonald's restaurants. I operate six now, but the highlight of my career was being a co-founder of the third Ronald McDonald House in the country; we now have some 225 worldwide.

But the third one was tough because people still didn't know what the Ronald McDonald House was about. Because it had the name McDonald's attached to it, it was very, very hard raising money . . . people thought if it's McDonald's they must have all the money they need. We just celebrated its twentieth year of operation and are now in a capital campaign to raise $7 million for a brand new house that will have thirty-one rooms.

Our present house has sixteen rooms. We've served over 40,000 families during that time, and the new house will double our capacity.

The Ronald McDonald House is a temporary home for families who have particular medical needs for their children. In a lot of cases it's cancer, burns, anything that is a medical interruption to the family. They come to the Ronald McDonald House because for the most part these are very young children. They identify with Ronald McDonald. It's an environment that they're familiar with, and it's on a very limited-needs basis, but it's low cost. In case of families that can't pay for it, it is free; others pay eight dollars a night. I'm very, very happy to be a part of it.

The turning point for me was that twelve-cent night. The realization it couldn't get any worse. I was dedicated. I was focused. Again, self-disciplined. Why would you go to the bank for twelve cents? Because that's the way you do it. If you're self-disciplined, you don't change what you're doing.

There was a very strong motivation to make this thing right for my father. When we sold our three restaurants in Cleveland, he stayed there and retired a millionaire. So I went from that twelve-cent day to making him a millionaire, and was able to make enough money to continue my career to financial independence. A warm, wonderful, fulfilling life.

Epilogue

World War I, and its aftermath, determined the course of the twentieth century. The communist takeover of Russia, the Versailles Treaty, the destruction of old empires and the creation of new European states, and the Depression created a petri dish of conflict.

The force of the Depression significantly contributed to the political, social, and military catastrophe that helped bring Hitler to power, encouraged Mussolini to dream ruinous dreams, created the opening for the military in Japan, and helped to seal Russia in a nightmare lasting decades.

The Great Depression tested the character and resolve of the democracies, and they failed. Britain and France accommodated Hitler at every turn, ultimately fashioning the paradigm of appeasement: the Munich Agreement. American foreign policy is still influenced by this unfortunate experience.

America, disillusioned after World War I, steered a course of isolation. Surrendering to geographical illusions and inadequate military preparedness, we created a second-rate military establishment. Britain and France also refused to allocate the proper resources to their military, and instead of opposing the dictators, they appeased them. Hitler built-up his military, successfully combating the Depression through rearmament, establishing himself a hero to his countrymen and intimidating the democracies. This, and his Realpolitik, changed the balance of power in 1930s Europe.

Hitler miscalculated—understandably, based on the lack of resolve shown by the democracies—and invaded Poland on September 1,

1939. Britain and France traded one wolf at the door—the Depression—for another—war. But Hitler was now irreversibly at war with the West, and his fate was sealed.

Twenty-seven months later, on December 7, 1941, the Japanese attacked Pearl Harbor, and America's isolationism ended. This was the penultimate event in our loss of innocence. November 22, 1963, would forever cast us into cynicism and suspicion.

At the conclusion of World War II, we were a colossus militarily and economically. Unscathed, we were the only nation with the atomic bomb, fully recovered from the Great Depression, prepared to dominate the remainder of the twentieth century. The world had become bipolar: the free world, led by the United States, and the forces of communism, led by Russia, both determined to establish their respective systems for the world to follow.

Russia had the atomic bomb by September 1949; we were now face to face with a country that for hundreds of years had expressed itself in violence. Difficult times would follow.

Although the East-West conflict devoured much time and energy, we had other concerns: racial conflict, a changing culture, political upheavals, the fall of communism, the technological revolution, and incredible prosperity, making the period from 1941 to the present the most exciting in our history.

America has learned to master change, the reason we have prospered and endured. We have survived World War II, the Cold War, poor leadership, and cultural crisis. We have kept jobs, started companies, raised families, and paid bills.

Some have failed. Most have succeeded. There are no final victories, and we take it one day at a time. So far we have done very well.

Index

A

D

E

O

P

S